NEW TESTAMENT STUDIES

NEW TESTAMENT STUDIES

by

C. H. DODD

Professor Emeritus in the University of Cambridge

MANCHESTER UNIVERSITY PRESS

Published by the University of Manchester
at
THE UNIVERSITY PRESS
316–324, OXFORD ROAD
MANCHESTER, 13
1953

PREFACE

I HAVE collected here eight papers written in the course of some twenty years upon various topics all falling within the field of New Testament studies.

The first three are contributions from various angles to an enterprise which has occupied much of the attention of students in this field during the period covered—the attempt to identify and describe the pre-literary tradition lying behind the Four Gospels. No. 3 links itself also with the two following papers, which return to a much-worked field, and represent one more attempt to become acquainted with the fascinating yet elusive workings of the mind which partly reveals itself in the epistles of Paul. The remaining three papers fall within the scope of biblical theology of the New Testament.

All eight papers have previously appeared in print, though not all are readily accessible. Nos. 2, 4 and 5 were originally published in the *Bulletin of the John Rylands Library* by the publishers of the present book. For permission to reprint Nos. 1 and 3 I am indebted to the publishers of the *Expository Times*, Messrs. T. & T. Clark. No. 6, which first appeared in *Theology*, was reissued as a pamphlet by the S.P.C.K., and I am particularly grateful for their courteous permission to include it here. No. 7 was printed in the *Harvard Divinity School Annual*. A small number of offprints (not more than thirty, I believe) were distributed in this country with the imprint of the Oxford University Press, whose consent I have obtained for this wider re-publication. No. 8 appeared in the *Official Register* of Harvard University, and is now published in this country for the first time.

All eight papers are reprinted virtually in their original form. I have corrected misprints, made some slight verbal changes, and omitted a few sentences which no longer seemed pertinent. But I have made no attempt to bring them up to date.   In two or three cases I am aware that the discussion has moved on since I wrote, but I believe the considerations here adduced are still not altogether irrelevant.

C. H. D.

CAMBRIDGE,
June 17, 1952.

CONTENTS

1. THE FRAMEWORK OF THE GOSPEL NARRATIVE

(1932)

THE criticism of the Gospels has achieved at least one secure result. Scarcely anyone now doubts that Mark is our primary Gospel. It offers the earliest extant narrative of the Ministry of Jesus Christ. The general order of that narrative reappears substantially in Matthew and Luke ; and even in the Fourth Gospel, which offers at first sight a totally different arrangement of events, traces of the Marcan order can be recognized. Thus the question is important, whether this earliest extant narrative can be trusted to give, if not a complete record, at least a record which so far as it goes follows the chronological order of events, and so enables us to trace the development of the Ministry. That this is the case is the assumption which underlies many of the modern ' lives ' of Jesus. It has, however, been challenged by recent critics. Dr. Rawlinson,[1] for example, in the Introduction to his Commentary on Mark, writes :

It is the conviction of the present editor, as the Commentary will make plain, that no such developments are to be traced, and that such attempts to treat the Marcan arrangement of the Gospel materials as supplying an outline, in chronological order, of the course of events, are profoundly mistaken ;

and again :

The most fundamental difficulty of all with regard to the ' Marcan hypothesis ' is just the intrinsic improbability of anything like a chronological outline of our Lord's Ministry, or an itinerary of His movements, having been preserved, throughout a whole generation of oral tradition, by a Church which was not primarily interested in such matters. It appears to be the clear upshot of the investigations to which reference

---
[1] Now (1953) Bishop of Derby.

has been made . . . that it is just the framework and the arrangement of the materials in our Gospels which ought to be set down to the account of the Evangelists, the materials themselves being derived from tradition.

The ' investigations ' to which Dr. Rawlinson refers are chiefly those of the German school of *Formgeschichte*, and in particular of Professor Karl Ludwig Schmidt, whose book, *Der Rahmen der Geschichte Jesu* (' The Framework of the Story of Jesus '), is the most thorough treatment of this subject that has appeared.

Professor Schmidt's thesis is that the Gospel according to Mark is compiled out of separate *pericopæ*, each transmitted as an independent unit in the folk-tradition of the Church (a typical example is the Leper story in Mark i. 40-45). The arrangement of these *pericopæ* is the work of the Evangelist, who in arranging them has had little regard for chronology or topography, but groups them in the main according to the topics with which they deal, or the features of the Ministry which they illustrate. Only where some *datum* in the story itself anchors it to a particular place —as for example, the appearance of a Syrophœnician woman anchors Mark vii. 24-30 to ' the borders of Tyre ' —can we accept a topographical setting. Similar internal indications of time scarcely exist until we reach the Passion narrative at the close, so that there is no secure basis for a chronology.

Apart from the arrangement, and the insertion of such insignificant connecting words as εὐθύς and πάλιν, the work of the Evangelist himself is to be recognized in the composition of short generalizing summaries (*Sammelberichte*), which punctuate the narrative, help the transition from one *pericope* to another, and remind the reader that the particular incidents narrated in detail are episodes in a widely extended ministry. These summaries can be recognized by their contrast in manner and content to the traditional narrative units. They lack the concreteness and particularity of the *pericopæ*. They relate nothing which belongs to one point of space and time to the exclusion of all other times and places. Their verbs are more often in the imperfect, the tense of continuous or habitual action, than in the aorist, the tense of action at a definite point. While the traditional units possess a high historical value, the *Sammelberichte* are mere ' framework ', and are not to be taken seriously as a contribution to our knowledge of the course of the Ministry.

Professor Schmidt seems to have made out his case that the main stuff of the Gospel is reducible to short narrative units, and that the framework is superimposed upon these units. But it seems worth while to inquire whether the order in which the units appear is indeed quite arbitrary, and the framework nothing more than an artificial construction of the Evangelist.

First, Professor Schmidt himself admits certain qualifications to this theory that the Evangelist's materials came to him solely in the form of isolated *pericopæ*. In some portions of the Gospel he recognizes comparatively large blocks which must have reached the Evangelist in substantially their present form. Thus the whole Passion-narrative, xiv–xvi, he thinks took form as a continuous whole long before Mark incorporated it in his work. Similarly, he recognizes as a single whole the story of the Sabbath at Capernaum, i. 23–38, which consists of four *pericopæ*, one of them approximating to the character of a *Sammelbericht*. Not only, he thinks, did it reach the Evangelist in this form, but things actually happened so. Again, he thinks it probable that two further complexes received their present continuous form at an earlier stage of the tradition —one consisting of the Storm, the Gadarene Swine, Jairus's Daughter, and the Hæmorrhoussa ; the other of the Feeding of the Multitude, the Voyage and the Landing (vi. 34–53, repeated in viii. 1–10). In these cases, however, he will not admit that the complexes represent an original historical sequence.

Further, in the central portion of the Gospel, where notes of place are most frequent, Professor Schmidt repeatedly refers to ' fragments ' or ' wreckage ' (*Bruchstücke*,

Trümmer) of an itinerary. I am not quite clear what he means by this. Sometimes he speaks as though the wealth of local indications reflected some real memory of journeyings in particular districts, which *might* have given rise to a formal itinerary ; at other times as though some such itinerary had once existed, but had been disintegrated by the Evangelist. I should say myself that if a narrative started with the words ἐκεῖθεν δὲ ἀναστάς, or the like (vii. 24, ix. 30, x. 1), even the simplest of the simple-minded early Christians would have been disposed to ask πόθεν ; in other words, such narratives can hardly have been wholly independent in the tradition. Either they came down linked with other *pericopæ*, or those who heard them told had some kind of outline itinerary in their minds, to which they readily related the separate stories. In any case, some modification of the strict theory of wholly independent units must be admitted. If we should infer that some ancient and traditional itinerary really lies behind the record of journeys in the North, then clearly such an itinerary cannot have been transmitted by itself, or for its own sake, but only as a part of an outline of the Ministry as a whole.

Once again, the theory that the arrangement has been determined by topical considerations calls for critical examination. The clearest case is the series of stories of conflicts with the scribes and Pharisees (ii. 1–iii. 6). But this series Professor Schmidt himself is disposed to regard as having been formed in the tradition before Mark worked upon it. In that case it tells us nothing of Mark's own method of arrangement. In the next great section, iii. 7–vi. 13, the dominant motive, dictating the arrangement of the material, is, according to Professor Schmidt, the πώρωσις, or hardening, of the people, with the allied motive of the ' Messianic secret '. It is true that this double theme is prominent from time to time in this section ; but it appears also in other sections, and even more strongly ; and Professor Schmidt himself admits that it is difficult to trace it in all *pericopæ* of this section. This fact he accounts for on the ground that Mark, having decided to place here some one particular *pericope* bearing upon the main theme of the section, took over along with it other material *already* connected with it in the tradition, connected with it, therefore, by links not merely topical. In the two sections which follow, the supposed dominant theme is certainly more consistently prominent : vi. 14–viii. 26 does deal with the theme : Jesus among the Gentiles ; and viii. 27–x. 45 is dominated by the thought of the approaching Passion. But even here the topical unity of the sections is not absolute. The refusal of a sign and the saying about leaven (viii. 11–15) have no direct bearing upon the theme ' to the Jew first and also to the Greek ' ; and it is difficult to bring the discussion of Divorce (x. 2–12) under Professor Schmidt's rubric, ' Jesus and His Disciples : The Imminent Passion '.

But apart from such qualifications, we may legitimately ask, Is this association of narratives dominated by a particular motive necessarily artificial or arbitrary ? Let us put it in this way : Was there, or was there not, a point in the life of Jesus at which He summoned His followers to accompany Him to Jerusalem with the prospect of suffering and death ? Is it, or is it not, likely that from that point on His thought and His speech dwelt with especial emphasis upon the theme of this approaching Passion ? Surely it is on every account likely. Thus, if one particular section of the Gospel is dominated by that theme, it is not because Mark has arbitrarily assembled from all quarters isolated *pericopæ* referring to the approaching Passion, but because these *pericopæ* originally and intrinsically belong to this particular phase of the Ministry. Again, was there, or was there not, a period in the life of Jesus when the outstanding feature of the situation was the obduracy of the people of Galilee ? That there was, we have the best authority for stating. A ' Q ' saying, accepted by Professor Schmidt as unquestionably genuine, represents Jesus as upbraiding the citizens of Capernaum, Bethsaida, and Chorazin because they did not repent.

This utterance clearly belongs to some particular occasion, and it looks back on a period of unfruitful work in Galilee which is now regarded as closed. Thus the theme of the πώρωσις of the people lies in the facts themselves, as they were in a particular phase of the Ministry.

To sum up : the theory of arrangement under topical rubrics is on the one hand not a sufficient explanation of the order of the Gospel, and on the other hand it is often not needed as an explanation, since the units have an inner connection with one another grounded in the facts themselves.

We may now make a fresh start by considering some of those passages which Professor Schmidt regards as the most characteristic elements in the framework supplied by the Evangelist himself—the *Sammelberichte*, or generalizing summaries which serve as links between the separate episodes in that portion of the Gospel where there is least inner connection between them. Professor Schmidt includes here :

i. 14–15.	Summary of the Galilæan Ministry.
i. 21–22.	Capernaum : Teaching with Authority.
i. 39.	Tour of Galilæan Synagogues.
ii. 13.	By the Sea.
iii. 7b–19.	Concourse of People ; Retirement to Hill-country ; Appointment of the Twelve.
iv. 33–34.	Parabolic Teaching.
vi. 7. 12–13.	Mission of the Twelve.
vi. 30.	Return of the Twelve.

The most remarkable of these passages is iii. 7b–19. Professor Schmidt seems to be clearly right in regarding this whole passage as a generalizing summary. The characteristic features of the narrative *pericopæ* are absent. We have two bald and general descriptions of stages in the Ministry : first, a stage of public teaching by the seashore ; and secondly, a stage in which Jesus is in retirement in the hill-country with a select number of disciples. No single and definite act is narrated in such a way that we can visualize it as happening on a particular day in a particular place. The verbs are mostly in the present or imperfect tense. The nucleus of each of the two descriptions is a dry catalogue of names—names of the districts from which people flocked to Jesus, and names of the Twelve Apostles. Thus we have before us a typical example of the kind of thing which Professor Schmidt attributes to the Evangelist's own composition. But what can have been his motive in composing it? It does not help to give continuity to the narrative, or to link the preceding *pericope* with that which follows. Nothing in iii. 7b–19 leads up to or prepares for the situation in iii. 20, which, in fact, does not differ from the situation in ii. 1–iii. 6. A boat is mentioned but nothing is done with it until ch. iv. Twelve apostles are mentioned, but they play no part until ch. vi. If Mark composed the passage as part of the framework of his narrative, he has done his work very clumsily.

But now let us put together these generalizing summaries, as Professor Schmidt has marked them. We may neglect iv. 33–34, as belonging rather to an account of Jesus's methods of teaching than to the narrative framework. The remaining summary passages read as follows (with the imperfect tenses emphasized in translation) :

After John's arrest Jesus came into Galilee proclaiming the Kingdom of God in the words, ' The time is fulfilled, and the Kingdom of God has drawn near : repent and believe in the Gospel.' And He enters [1] into Capernaum ; and on Sabbath days He would go to synagogue and teach. And all were in a state of astonishment at His teaching ; for He was wont to teach them as one with authority, and not like the scribes. And He went proclaiming in the synagogues throughout Galilee, and casting out demons. And He went out to the seaside, and the whole crowd would come to Him, and He would teach them. And from Judæa and Jerusalem, from Idumæa and Peræa, and the districts of Tyre and Sidon, a great throng, hearing what He was doing, came to Him.

---

[1] Mark i. 21, following some MSS. in reading εἰσπορεύεται, with Schmidt.

And He told His disciples to have a boat waiting for Him because of the crowds, so that they should not throng Him ; for He healed many, so that all who had plagues kept pressing upon Him to touch Him. And the foul fiends, whenever they saw Him, would fall before Him, and cry out, ' Thou art the Son of God.' And He would enjoin them not to make Him known. And He goes up into the hill-country, and summons those whom He Himself wanted, and they came to Him. And He appointed Twelve that they might be with Him and that He might send them out to preach and to have authority to expel demons. So He appointed the Twelve, and gave Simon the name of Peter ; and James son of Zebedee and John his brother ; and to them He gave the name Boanerges, i.e. Thundermen ; and Andrew and Philip and Bartholomew and Matthew and Thomas and James son of Alpheus and Thaddæus and Simon the Cananæan and Judas Iscariot His betrayer. And He summons the Twelve and began to send them out two by two ; and He used to give them authority over foul fiends ; and they went out and preached repentance. They kept expelling many demons and anointing many sick folk with oil and healing them. And the apostles gather to Jesus and reported to Him all that they had done and said.

The striking thing here is the way in which the summaries fall naturally into something very like a continuous narrative. We have in fact obtained, merely by putting them together, a perspicuous outline of the Galilæan Ministry, forming a framework into which the separate pictures are set. So continuous a structure scarcely arose out of casual links supplied here and there where the narrative seemed to demand it. But we may raise the further question, whether it is the independent work of the Evangelist at all. The outline gives a conspectus of the Galilæan Ministry in three stages : A. Synagogue preaching and exorcism in Capernaum and elsewhere ; B. Teaching, healing, and exorcism by the seashore, in the presence of vast crowds from all Palestine and beyond ; C. Retirement in the Hill-country with a small circle of disciples, who are sent on preaching and healing tours.

This is the frame into which the pictures (the narrative *pericopæ*) are to be fitted. But they fit very ill. Under rubric A we have only two examples of visits to synagogues ; the third synagogue episode comes much later on. With rubric B the case is better, for many of the incidents in iv–vi are actually staged on or near the seashore. If this group had followed immediately upon iii. 11 the picture would have fitted the frame at this point ; but actually the series of seashore stories is separated from its proper rubric by the third rubric, ' He goes up to the hill-country ', as well as by the twofold episode iii. 20–35, which has no proper setting in the framework. The third rubric is actually an empty one, for there is no particular incident which has its setting in a retirement to the hill-country.

Now if you have in hand a set of pictures, and desire to frame them, you construct a frame to fit the pictures ; but if you have in hand a set of pictures *and a frame*, not designed to fit one another, you must fit them as best you can, and the result may be something of a botch. Thus it seems likely that in addition to materials in *pericope* form, Mark had an outline, itself also traditional, to which he attempted to work, with incomplete success.

But Professor Schmidt and Dr. Rawlinson think there is some ' intrinsic improbability' in the idea that oral tradition transmitted an outline of the Ministry of Jesus in chronological order. As against this, we may note that Professor Martin Dibelius, in his *Formgeschichte des Evangeliums*, has pointed to summary outlines of the life of Jesus embedded in the primitive preaching of the Church, appearing in various speeches in the Acts of the Apostles. Fragments of such an outline he recognizes also in I Cor. xv. 3–7 and xi. 23–25. The evidence, he observes, does not suggest that any one outline was universal, but it does suggest that some kind of outline formed a regular part of the *kerygma* everywhere. The fullest examples of such primitive *kerygma* that we possess are those of Acts x. 37–41 and Acts xiii. 23–31. The former passage gives the scheme : preaching of John ; baptism of Jesus ; beginning of the

B

Ministry in Galilee ; healing and exorcism ; change of scene to Jerusalem ; crucifixion and resurrection. The latter passage contains a much fuller account of the preaching of John at the beginning, and of the Resurrection at the close. Its record of the Ministry is much slighter, but it establishes a journey in company with disciples from Galilee to Jerusalem, ending with the death of Jesus.

In view of this evidence, I cannot see any intrinsic improbability in the supposition that the primitive Church did transmit an outline of the Ministry of Jesus, with some regard at least to its topographical and chronological setting. The outline which we have recognized as existing in fragmentary form in the framework of Mark may well have belonged to a form of the primitive *kerygma*. It implies a somewhat more elaborate form of it than those which are preserved in the Acts of the Apostles ; but these, no doubt, are summaries of summaries.

I submit, therefore, that we are led to conceive the materials which Mark took over from tradition as being of three kinds :

(i) Isolated independent *pericopæ*, handed down without any connection ;

(ii) Larger complexes, which again may be of various kinds : genuinely continuous narratives ; *pericopæ* strung upon an itinerary ; *pericopæ* connected by unity of theme.

(iii) An outline of the whole ministry, designed, perhaps, as an introduction to the Passion-story, but serving also as a background of reference for separate stories ; fragments of this survive in the framework of the Gospel.

In shaping these materials into a Gospel, Mark has attempted to work to the traditional outline, but he is embarrassed by two facts : (*a*) the outline was far too meagre to provide a setting for all the detailed narratives at his disposal, while on the other hand it referred to phases of the Ministry not illustrated by the detailed narratives ; (*b*) the materials were already partially grouped in ways which cut across a truly chronological order. Thus he was faced by a difficult problem. I suggest he has solved it, though not wholly satisfactorily, by a compromise between a chronological and a topical order. Where the outline gave a clue to the setting of particular narrative units or groups of units, he has arranged them accordingly. Where groups of narrative units came down to him already arranged topically, he allowed the arrangement to stand, relating the first member of the group (e.g. ii. 1–12, the first conflict-story) to what appeared to be its most suitable point in the outline scheme. When he was left with wholly disconnected units on his hands, he found place for them as best he could, being sometimes guided by topical considerations, sometimes by a sense of the chronological stage to which the particular episode seemed most naturally to belong. Thus we need not be so scornful of the Marcan order as has recently become the fashion, though we shall not place in it the implicit confidence it once enjoyed. It is in large measure, as Professor Schmidt argues, the result of the Evangelist's own work, rather than directly traditional. But he did that work not arbitrarily or irresponsibly, but under such guidance as he could find in tradition. It is hazardous to argue from the precise sequence of the narrative in detail ; yet there is good reason to believe that in broad lines the Marcan order does represent a genuine succession of events, within which movement and development can be traced.

2. A NEW GOSPEL

(1936)

THE Trustees of the British Museum have recently published the text of four small fragments of papyrus in their possession, which represent three leaves of a codex (i.e. a bound volume as distinct from a roll). They are now numbered *Egerton Papyrus 2* in the British Museum collection. The text is admirably edited with introduction and commentary by Mr. H. Idris Bell[1] and Mr. T. C. Skeat, in a volume entitled *Fragments of an Unknown Gospel and Other Early Christian Papyri* (1935). The editors have since issued a revised text under the title *The New Gospel Fragments*.

The editors discuss at length the date of the papyrus, and come to the conclusion that it belongs to the middle of the second century. They are able to cite the concurrence of other experts with their conclusion. As I am no palæographer, I shall not join in the discussion, but assume that the papyrus was written at a date not far removed in either direction from A.D. 150. If so, then it is probably the earliest piece of Christian writing known, with the single exception of the still more recently published Rylands papyrus of the Fourth Gospel (P. Ryl. Gk. 457), of which I shall have something to say presently.

The text of the papyrus is reprinted here (by permission) after the revised form given in Bell and Skeat, *The New Gospel Fragments*.

Fragment 1 *verso*]

. . . .

$$]\iota \, . \, [(1) \, ? \, \delta \, \delta\grave{\varepsilon}]$$
$$['I(\eta\sigma o\tilde{v}\varsigma) \, \varepsilon\tilde{\iota}\pi\varepsilon\nu] \, \tau o\tilde{\iota}\varsigma \, \nu o\mu\iota\kappa o[\tilde{\iota}\varsigma \cdot \, \kappa o\lambda\acute{a}\text{-}]$$
$$[\zeta\varepsilon\tau\varepsilon \, \pi\acute{a}]\nu\tau\alpha \, \tau\grave{o}\nu \, \pi\alpha\varrho\alpha\pi\varrho\acute{a}\sigma\sigma[o\nu\tau\alpha]$$
$$[\kappa\alpha\grave{\iota} \, \check{a}\nu o]\mu o\nu \, \kappa\alpha\grave{\iota} \, \mu\grave{\eta} \, \grave{\varepsilon}\mu\acute{\varepsilon} \cdot \, \varepsilon[\grave{\iota} \, \gamma]\alpha\varrho \, . \, .$$

---

[1] Now (1953) Sir Harold Bell.

5 [. . .? νο]μοποιεῖ, πῶς ποιε[ῖ·] (2) πρὸς
[δὲ τοὺς] ἄ[ρ]χοντας τοῦ λαοῦ [στ]ρα-
[φεὶς εἶ]πεν τὸν λόγον τοῦτο[ν·] ἐραυ-
[νᾶτε τ]ὰς γραφάς· ἐν αἷς ὑμεῖς δο-
[κεῖτε] ζωὴν ἔχειν ἐκεῖναί εἰ[σ]ιν
10 [αἱ μαρτ]υροῦσαι περὶ ἐμοῦ· (3) μὴ δ[ο-]
[κεῖτε ὅ]τι ἐγὼ ἦλθον κατηγο[ρ]ῆσαι
[ὑμῶν] πρὸς τὸν π(ατέ)ρα μου· ἔστιν
[ὁ κατη]γορῶν ὑμῶν Μω(ϋσῆς) εἰς ὃν
[ὑμεῖς] ἠλπίκατε· (4) α[ὐ]τῶν δὲ λε-
15 [γόντω]ν ε[ὖ] οἴδαμεν ὅτι Μω(ϋσεῖ) ἐλά-
[λησεν] ὁ θ(εό)ς[·] σὲ δὲ οὐκ οἴδαμεν
[πόθεν εἶ]· ἀποκριθεὶς ὁ Ἰη(σοῦς) εἶ-
[πεν αὐτο]ῖς· νῦν κατηγορεῖται
[ὑμῶν ἡ ἀ]πιστεί[α
20 ? ἀ]λλο . [
] . [

. . . .

Fragment 1 recto]

. . . .

(5) ? ἔ]λκω[σιν] β[αστάσαν-]
[τες δὲ] λίθους ὁμοῦ λι[θάζω-]
σι[ν αὐ]τόν· (6) καὶ ἐπέβαλον [τὰς]
25 χεῖ[ρας] αὐτῶν ἐπ᾽ αὐτὸν οἱ [ἄρχον-]
τες [ἵ]να πιάσωσιν καὶ παρ[αδώ-]
σω[σι]ν τῷ ὄχλῳ· καὶ οὐκ ἠ[δύναντο]
αὐτὸν πιάσαι ὅτι οὔπω ἐ[ληλύθει]
αὐτοῦ ἡ ὥρα τῆς παραδό[σεως]
30 (7) αὐτὸς δέ ὁ κ(ύριο)ς ἐξελθὼν [ἐκ τῶν χει-]
ρῶν ἀπένευσεν ἀπ᾽ [αὐτῶν·]
(8) καὶ [ἰ]δοὺ λεπρὸς προσελθ[ὼν αὐτῷ]
λέγει· διδάσκαλε Ἰη(σοῦ) λε[προῖς συν-]
οδεύων καὶ συνεσθίω[ν αὐτοῖς]
35 ἐν τῷ πανδοχείῳ ἐλ[έπρησα]
καὶ αὐτὸς ἐγώ· ἐὰν [ο]ὖν [σὺ θέλῃς]
καθαρίζομαι· (9) ὁ δὴ κ(ύριο)ς [ἔφη αὐτῷ]
θέλ[ω] καθαρίσθητι· [καὶ εὐθέως]

[ἀ]πέστη ἀπ' αὐτοῦ ἡ λέπ[ρα· (10) ὁ δὲ κ(ύριο)ς]
40 [εἶπεν αὐτῷ] πορε[υθεὶς ἐπίδει-]
[ξον σεαυτὸ]ν τοῖ[ς ἱερεῦσι

·   ·   ·   ·   ·   ·   ·

Fragment 2 recto]

[   ].

(11) νόμενοι πρὸς αὐτὸν ἐξ[ετασ-]
τικῶς ἐπείραζον αὐτὸν λ[έγοντες]
45 διδάσκαλε 'Ιη(σοῦ) οἴδαμεν ὅτι [ἀπὸ θ(εο)ῦ]
ἐλήλυθας ἃ γὰρ ποιεῖς μα[ρτυρεῖ]
ὑπὲρ το[ὺ]ς προφ(ήτ)ας πάντας [(12) εἰπὲ οὖν]
ἡμεῖν· ἐξὸν τοῖς βα(σι)λεῦσ[ιν ἀποδοῦ-]
ναι τὰ ἀν[ή]κοντα τῇ ἀρχῇ ἀπ[οδῶμεν αὐ-]
50 τοῖς ἢ μ[ή] (13) ὁ δὲ 'Ιη(σοῦς) εἰδὼς [τὴν δι-]
άνοιαν [αὐτ]ῶν ἐμβρειμ[ησάμενος]
εἶπεν α[ὐτοῖς·] τί με καλεῖτ[ε τῷ στό-]
ματι ὑμ[ῶν δι]δάσκαλον· μ[ὴ ἀκού-]
οντες ὃ [λ]έγω· (14) καλῶς Ἡ[σ(αΐ)ας περὶ ὑ-]
55 μῶν ἐπ[ρο]φ(ήτευ)σεν εἰπών· ὁ [λαὸς οὗ-]
τος τοῖς [χείλ]εσιν αὐτ[ῶν τιμῶσιν
με ἡ [δὲ καρδί]α αὐτῷ[ν πόρρω ἀπέ-]
χει ἀπ' ἐ[μοῦ μ]άτη[ν με σέβονται]
ἐντάλ[ματα

·   ·   ·   ·   ·   ·   ·

43. sc. παραγενόμενοι (παραγε on the preceding page).

Fragment 2 verso]

60 (15) [. . . . . .]τῳ τόπῳ [κ]ατακλεισαν-
[. . . . .] ὑποτέτακτα[ι] ἀδήλως
[. . . . . .]εται τὸ βάρος αὐτοῦ ἄστατο(ν)
[. . . . .] (16) ἀπορηθέντων δὲ ἐκεί-
[νων ὡς] πρὸς τὸ ξένον ἐπερώτημα·
65 [? τότε π]εριπατῶν ὁ 'Ιη(σοῦς) [ἐ]στάθη
[ἐπὶ τοῦ] χείλους τοῦ 'Ιο[ρδ]άνου
[ποταμ]οῦ καὶ ἐκτείνα[ς τὴν] χεῖ-
[ρα αὐτο]ῦ τὴν δεξιὰν [. . .]μισεν
[. . . . . κ]αὶ κατέσπειρ[εν ἐπ]ὶ τὸν

70 [. . . . . .]ον· (17) καὶ τότε [. . . .] κατε-
    [? σπαρμ]ένον ὕδωρ· ἐ . [. .] . ν τὴν
    [. . . . .]· καὶ ἐπ . [. .]θη ἐνώ-
    [πιον αὐτῶν ἐ]ξήγα[γ]εν [δὲ] καρπὸ(ν)
    [. . . . .]πολλ[. . . . . .] εἰς χα-
75 [ρὰν ? . . . .]τα[. . . . . .]υτους·

      ·   ·   ·   ·   ·   ·   ·   ·   ·

Fragment 3 *verso*]

76   ] . παρη
                                ]ς ἐὰν
                                ] αὐτοῦ
                                ]ημενος
80   ]εἰδὼς
                                ηπ.

      ·   ·   ·   ·   ·   ·   ·   ·   ·

Fragment 3 *recto*]

      ἕν ἐσμ[εν
      μένω π[λί-]
      θους εἰς [ἀπο-]
85   κτείνω[σιν αὐτὸν
      λέγει· ο[
      [.]ε[. .] . . [

      ·   ·   ·   ·   ·   ·   ·   ·   ·

Fragment 4 *recto*]   Blank
Fragment 4 *verso*]   ]σ[

The text of the papyrus deals throughout, like our
canonical Gospels, with stories and sayings of Jesus. Its
contents are as follows :

Fragment 1, *verso*, contains part of a controversy between
Jesus and ' lawyers ' and ' rulers of the people '.

Fragment 1, *recto*, contains (*a*) the conclusion of a story
in which Jesus escapes from an attack on His life ; this
may have been the sequel to the controversy reported
above ; and (*b*) a story of the healing of a leper, practically
complete.

Fragment 2, *recto*, gives an account of a question asked by Jesus, and of His reply. So much is clear, but the actual text of the question has to be restored conjecturally, and the reply, though clear so far as it goes, is incomplete.

Fragment 2, *verso*, gives the remains of a question asked by Jesus, and goes on to relate something that He did ; but here the papyrus is so badly broken that it is difficult to restore either the question or the story with any certainty.

Fragment 3, which is very exiguous, seems to be a remnant of another story about an attempt on the life of Jesus.

Fragment 4 is a mere scrap, on which the editors can read only a single letter.

It is clear that we have here the same kind of material that we have in the canonical Gospels. The document, whatever it was, seems to have been made up of comparatively short sections, each of which contained a narrative about Jesus or a dialogue between Him and other persons, or a mixture of narrative and dialogue. It is fortunate that we have in Fragment 1 *recto* the close of one section and the beginning of another, because the way in which the sections are placed in relation to one another shows the way in which the document was constructed. The former section closes with the words, ' The Lord Himself, going out from their hands, departed from them.' The episode is thus dismissed, and the next section begins, without any connecting or introductory matter, ' And behold a leper approaching Him said . . . '. We conclude that the author took over, from some source or other, sections which were complete in themselves, and placed them in succession, without any attempt, so far as the MS. shows, to weave them into a continuous narrative. That is not to say that the document was a mere cento or anthology. The compilation of the Synoptic Gospels seems to have proceeded on a similar method. In all of them, indeed, there is at times an attempt to supply continuity between the sections—least in Mark, most in Luke —but in no case has the attempt been carried through. It is one of the points made by recent criticism that the characteristic method of Gospel compilation was just this artless collocation of originally independent units, and that the more effort after continuity there is, the more advanced is the stage of development from the original tradition. But even the Fourth Gospel, though it departs more widely than the Synoptics from the traditional forms of Gospel composition, retains clear traces of the earlier method. We may say therefore that the present document has the distinctive marks of that type of literature known to us as ' Gospels ', so far as the treatment of the material goes. Whether in its complete state it had the unity imposed upon the material by the special aims which actuated our canonical evangelists, the fragments do not allow us to judge. But, provisionally, the editors seem justified in calling it ' an unknown Gospel '.

We may proceed to compare it with our extant Gospels, and first in respect of language.

The language of the papyrus is good Hellenistic Greek, with no trace, so far as I can see, of Semitism. There do not appear to be any peculiarities which would suggest an Aramaic original, such as appear to a greater or less degree in all the canonical Gospels. Nor, apart from actual citations of the Old Testament, does the language appear to betray the influence of the ' biblical Greek ' of the LXX, as the Lucan writings notably do in some places.

The vocabulary may be analysed as follows : [1]

A considerable number of words and locutions are naturally common to the papyrus and to all four Gospels, including such keywords as διδάσκαλος, κύριος, γραφαί (' Scriptures ' in the technical sense), πειράζειν, χεῖρας ἐπιβάλλειν, etc.

Of 37 significant words or locutions which are not thus common, (i) 10 are not found in the Gospels at all, or are found only in senses different from those of the papyrus. These are :

παραπράσσειν not in N.T.

παράδοσις = ' betrayal ', or ' arrest ', not in N.T.

[1] I have included in the list such restorations as seem reasonably certain.

ἀπονεύειν not in N.T., but ἐκνεύειν in the same sense
(= 'depart') in John.

λεπρεῖν (or λεπροῦν) not in N.T.

ἐξεταστικῶς not in N.T. ; the verb ἐξετάζειν in Matthew
and John.[1]

ἀνήκειν in Paul.

ἄστατος not in N.T.

ἐπερώτημα in I Peter ; the verb ἐπερωτᾶν very common
in the Synoptics, once (+ 1 *lect. dub.*) in John.

χεῖλος = 'edge' only in Hebrews.

κατασπείρειν not in N.T.

ἐξάγειν καρπόν not in N.T.

(ii) 10 are found in the Lucan writings but not in the
other Gospels.   These are :

ἄρχοντες τοῦ λαοῦ : the simple ἄρχοντες, of the Jewish
authorities, occurs 4 times in Luke, 3 times in
John, not in Matthew or Mark.

συνοδεύειν

συνεσθίειν

πανδοχεῖον

ἀφιστάναι = 'depart'.

παραγενόμενοι used as here very frequently in the Lucan
writings, and not elsewhere in N.T. ; the verb
παραγενέσθαι 28 times in Luke and Acts, 3 times
in Matthew, once in Mark, once in the genuine
text of John.

ἀρχή in political sense.

κατακλείειν

ὑποτάσσειν

ἄδηλος

and 4 are characteristically Lucan, though found rarely
in other Gospels, viz.

νομικός once in Matthew, 6 times in Luke (+ 1 *lect dub.*),
not in Mark or John.

στραφείς twice in Matthew, not in Mark, twice in John,
7 times in Luke (+ 1 *lect. dub.*).

---

[1] Also in the Oxyrhynchus *Sayings of Jesus*, Ox. Pap. 654.

ἀπορεῖν once (*lect. dub.*) in Mark, twice in Luke–Acts, once in John, not in Matthew.

(iii) 2 are found in John and in the Lucan writings, but not in Matthew or Mark, viz.

λιθάζειν 4 times in genuine text of John, twice in Acts.

πιάζειν 8 times in John, twice in Acts,

and 2 are relatively common in John and in the Lucan writings, but rare in Matthew and Mark, viz.

οὗτος ὁ λόγος once in Mark, twice (both *dub. lect.*) in Matthew, twice in Luke, 3 times in Acts, 3 times in John.[1]

μαρτυρεῖν not in Mark, once in Matthew, 33 times in John, 14 times in Lucan writings.

(iv) 4 are found in all the Synoptics, but not in John, viz.

λεπρός

λέπρα

καθαρίζειν

ἐκτείνας τὴν χεῖρα

and 2 in Matthew and the Lucan writings, but not in John, viz.

ἐπιδεικνύναι

βάρος.

(v) Of words or locutions which enter into the vocabulary of the Gospels 4 only are not found in the Lucan writings, viz.

ἐραυνᾶν twice in John, not in Synoptics.

ἀπιστία once in Matthew, twice in the genuine text of Mark, not in Luke or John.

ἐληλύθει ἡ ὥρα, or the like, once in Matthew (ἤγγικεν ἡ ὥρα), once in Mark (ἦλθεν ἡ ὥρα), 14 times in John.

ἐμβριμᾶσθαι once in Matthew, twice in Mark, twice in John.

The result of this analysis is to show that the new text

[1] The plural οὗτοι οἱ λόγοι is more common, but the emphatic use of the singular is characteristic.

has in respect of vocabulary a much closer affinity with the Lucan writings than with the Gospels according to Matthew, Mark, and John.   Out of the 27 significant terms which belong to the vocabulary both of the canonical Gospels and of the papyrus, all but 4 are Lucan, and no fewer than 17 are characteristic of 'Luke' as compared with the other Synoptics.

It does not necessarily follow that the writer of the new document was influenced by the Lucan writings, especially as the connections in which the words are used have seldom any close relation to their contexts in the Third Gospel. The latter is, among the Gospels, the most 'literary' in style, and the farthest removed from the relatively 'vulgar' Greek with an Aramaic colouring in which the evangelical record was originally written down. The document we are examining had, like the Lucan writings, a relatively literary or secular character. This is borne out by the occurrence of no fewer than 10 terms, in so small a fragment, which are strange to the vocabulary of the canonical Gospels, and by the absence of Semitism. We are here at an even further remove from the primitive Gospel-style, founded upon a reverence for the forms of the oral tradition.

A similar conclusion follows from a consideration of the manner of referring to Jesus. In narrative He is called either by name (ὁ Ἰησοῦς) or, 'the Lord' (ὁ κύριος). The former of these is usual in the primitive strata of the Synoptic Gospels ; the latter is confined (in narrative) to Luke and John. In the second-century Gospel according to Peter, we may observe, Jesus is always called ' the Lord '. Peculiar to the new document is the address διδάσκαλε Ἰησοῦ, which would represent ' Rabbi Jesus '. ' Rabbi ', or its Greek equivalent διδάσκαλε, is the usual form of address all through the Synoptic Gospels, and is found also in John. The vocative Ἰησοῦ is not common. It is absent from Matthew and John. It occurs 8 times in Mark, and on each occasion Luke has reproduced it ; and Luke adds one more example, in the mouth of the ' Penitent

Thief', xxiii. 42 ; this is actually the only case in the canonical Gospels where the vocative ' Jesus ' occurs by itself, without any further title accompanying it. It occurs also in the Gospel according to the Hebrews. The combination, ' Rabbi Jesus ', is unparalleled. It has been stated, since the publication of this papyrus, that this follows ancient Jewish usage, and may be regarded as possibly even more primitive than the forms of address used in the Synoptic Gospels. But this does not appear to be so. Teachers of the Law were addressed respectfully as ' Rabbi ' in the time of Jesus (Hillel seems to be the first of whom we have definite record), but the name was not added. Later, the respectful form of address was turned into a title, and eminent teachers were referred to as ' Rabbi Jochanan ', ' Rabbi Eliezer ', and so forth. This usage appears to have begun with the disciples of Jochanan ben Zakkai, after the fall of the Temple. But it does not appear to have been the custom to *address* a teacher in this way. The form of *address* was the simple ' Rabbi ', which is the διδάσκαλε of the Synoptic Gospels. The address ' Rabbi Jesus ' therefore does not correspond with contemporary Jewish usage, and in default of further evidence we must regard it as an imitative form arising in a circle not intimately acquainted with Jewish usages, but aware that Jewish teachers were referred to as ' Rabbi N. or M.'. In that case, the composition would probably belong to a period in which that usage was already established.

Our general conclusion so far is that the document before us was a composition similar to the canonical Gospels, resembling in its literary character the Third Gospel, and representing a stage of development away from the primitive Gospel-type at least as late as that. The date is in any case earlier than the middle of the second century, and it is probably later than the Lucan writings, and not earlier than the period (between the fall of the Temple and the Hadrianic War) in which the title (as distinct from the honorific form of address) ' Rabbi ' came into common use among the Jews.

We must now turn to an examination of the text in detail.

SECTION I.   FRAGMENT 1, *verso*, LINES 1–21

The opening sentences are fragmentary. All that is certain is that they were addressed by Jesus to ' lawyers '. I will leave them for the moment.   From line 6 the restoration seems fairly certain.   The text may be rendered as follows :

> Turning to the rulers of the people He spoke this saying : ' Search the Scriptures : those [Scriptures] in which you suppose that you have life are the ones which bear witness concerning me. Do not think I have come to accuse you to my Father : your accuser is Moses, on whom you have set your hope.' And when they said, ' We know well that God spoke to Moses, but we do not know whence you come,' Jesus said in reply, ' Now your unbelief is accused. . . .'

The following points are to be noted.

(i) The transitional formula στραφείς is characteristically Lucan, and it is a Lucan tendency also to distinguish between various groups addressed by Jesus.   Thus the ' anti-Pharisaic discourse ' is in Matthew addressed all through to ' scribes and Pharisees ', whereas in Luke the first four sayings are addressed to Pharisees, and then Jesus turns to the ' lawyers '.   Similarly here He first addresses the ' lawyers ' and then turns to the ' rulers of the people '.

(ii) The term ' rulers ' for the Jewish authorities is peculiar to John and the Lucan writings, and the full phrase ' rulers of the people ' occurs only in Acts iv. 8, where the Sanhedrin, consisting of ' rulers, elders and scribes ', is addressed as ' rulers of the people and elders '. In the papyrus the ' rulers of the people ' are distinguished from the ' lawyers ' (= scribes), and presumably represent the other categories of Sanhedrists, the ' rulers and elders ' of Acts.

(iii) The saying addressed to the ' rulers ' reads like John v. 39.   According to the Greek MSS. this verse reads, ' You search (or Search) the Scriptures, because you think that in them you have eternal life ; and it is they that bear witness concerning me.' But the ' Western Text ', as represented by the Old Latin MSS. *a* and *b*, and by the Curetonian Syriac, had the reading, ' those [scriptures] in which you think you have life are those which bear witness concerning me '. Turned into Greek, this would be identical with the text of the papyrus.

(iv) The second saying corresponds closely to John v. 45 : ' Do not think that I will accuse you to the Father. Your accuser is Moses, on whom you have set your hope.' There are only two variations : (*a*) the form ἦλθον κατηγορῆσαι for the future κατηγορήσω. The construction is found only once in the Fourth Gospel, iv. 7. John prefers the construction with ἵνα, e.g. xii. 47, οὐ γὰρ ἦλθον ἵνα κρίνω τὸν κόσμον. Ἦλθον with the infinitive, however, is not uncommon in other Gospels ; e.g. Matthew v. 17, ἦλθον καταλῦσαι τὸν νόμον, Mark x. 45, οὐκ ἦλθον διακονῆσαι, Gospel according to the Egyptians, ἦλθον καταλῦσαι τὰ ἔργα τῆς θηλείας, Ebionite Gospel, ἦλθον καταλῦσαι τὰς θυσίας. We may perhaps take it that the form ἦλθον *cum inf.* was more or less stereotyped in early Christian usage for the formulation of sayings of Jesus expressing the purpose of His incarnation. (*b*) The addition of μου after πατέρα, which is insignificant.

(v) The reply of the ' rulers ' is in terms of John ix. 29, with a pronoun transposed into the second person : ' We know that God spoke to Moses, but we do not know whence this man comes.' The only changes are (*a*) εὖ οἴδαμεν (a locution strange to the N.T.) for the simple οἴδαμεν, and (*b*) the aorist ἐλάλησεν for the perfect λελάληκεν, an improvement in literary style, for John's predilection for the perfect is excessive.

The passage before us therefore consists entirely of three ' Johannine ' sayings, two attributed to Jesus and one to the ' rulers '. The verbal resemblance is so close that we have only three possible explanations : (i) the papyrus quotes the Fourth Gospel ; (ii) John quotes from the ' Unknown Gospel ', or (iii) both go back to a common source.   To decide between these possibilities is a delicate matter.   The editors are disposed to reject (i), and to leave open the choice between (ii) and (iii).

The only tests we can apply are the following : (i) Is the language of this passage more characteristic of the papyrus as a whole, or of the Fourth Gospel as a whole ? (ii) Do the sayings form a more logical sequence in the papyrus or in their contexts in the Fourth Gospel ?

(i) The application of the first test must be somewhat precarious where the material to which it is to be applied is so scanty, and comparison is the more difficult because apart from the present passage the papyrus has preserved so few words of Jesus, from which the style of the sayings in the ' Unknown Gospel ' might be determined.   But the following observations may be made : (a) The verb ἐραυνᾶν is found in no Gospel but the Fourth.   (b) The expression ζωὴν ἔχειν is peculiarly Johannine, occurring 14 times in the Fourth Gospel, 4 times in I John, and nowhere else in the N.T.   (c) The verb μαρτυρεῖν is, as we have seen, highly characteristic of the Fourth Gospel, occurring 33 times ;   and μαρτυρεῖν περὶ τινός occurs 19 times there, and in no other Gospel.   (d) Ἐκεῖνος used as a pronoun is extremely common in the Fourth Gospel, occurring 50 times, as against 4 times in Matthew, twice in the genuine text of Mark, and 3 times in Luke.   In particular, the form ἐκεῖνός ἐστιν (ἦν, or the like) is frequent in the Fourth Gospel (i. 8, v. 35, ix. 37, x. 1, xiii. 26, xiv. 21), and absent from the others except Mark iv. 20.   The expression ἐν αἷς δοκεῖτε ζωὴν ἔχειν, ἐκεῖναί εἰσιν αἱ μαρτυροῦσαι may be compared with John xiv. 21, ὁ ἔχων τὰς ἐντολάς μου . . . ἐκεῖνός ἐστιν ὁ ἀγαπῶν με.   (e) The expression ἔστιν ὁ κατηγορῶν is of a type common in the Fourth Gospel, cf. v. 32, ἄλλος ἐστὶν ὁ μαρτυρῶν, viii. 18, ἐγώ εἰμι ὁ μαρτυρῶν, viii. 54, ἔστιν ὁ πατήρ μου ὁ δοξάζων με, ix. 37, vi. 33, vi. 64.   The articular participle is itself a construction for which the Fourth evangelist displays a certain predilection.   As it is twice used in this short passage of the papyrus, so it occurs 18 times in 2 pages

(in Nestlé's text) of John vi.   But the Fourth Gospel itself
is not uniform in this respect.   There are only 12 articular
participles in 6 pages of the Farewell Discourses, and only
6 in 2 pages of John vii.   (*f*) The words πόθεν εἶ refer to
a question much to the fore in the Fourth Gospel, and not
elsewhere ; cf. John vii. 27, τοῦτον οἴδαμεν πόθεν ἔστιν,
viii. 14, οἶδα πόθεν ἦλθον καὶ ποῦ ὑπάγω, ὑμεῖς δὲ οὐκ οἴδατε
πόθεν ἔρχομαι ἢ ποῦ ὑπάγω, xix. 9, πόθεν εἶ σύ.

The impression, therefore, which the whole passage produces, of being characteristically Johannine in language, is
borne out by an examination of the actual expressions used.
None of these expressions recurs in the papyrus.   They
may, of course, have occurred in other parts of the ' Unknown Gospel ', but of this we have no evidence.   On the
evidence before us we must say that while the papyrus as
a whole is linguistically most closely akin to the Lucan
writings, in this passage its language is Johannine through
and through.   The natural conclusion is that the passage
was taken by the author from a ' Johannine ' source.   If
we suppose that this source was one used also by the
Fourth Evangelist, we should have to say that the language
of the Fourth Gospel was coloured all through by this
hypothetical source, since the expressions we have examined have parallels in all parts of the Gospel.   The
easier hypothesis would be that the author of the ' Unknown Gospel ' borrowed from the Gospel according to
John.

(ii) The second test is necessarily more subjective, for
different readers will judge differently the logical coher-
ence of a given passage.   Here the editors judge that in
the papyrus ' there is a logical progression in the thought ',
and that ' the development is perfectly smooth and self-
consistent '.   But it may be questioned whether the progression would seem as logical as it does if the reader had
not unconsciously in mind the context supplied in the
Fourth Gospel.   The first two sayings occur in the discourse of John v, a large part of which is concerned with the
theme of ' testimony '.   Jesus appeals first to the testimony

c

of John the Baptist (v. 32–35). But this is not the chief or final testimony. God Himself bears testimony to His Son (v. 36–38). This testimony the Jews do not accept because ' you have not His word abiding in you '. This reference to the ' word of God ' introduces the saying ' You search the Scriptures . . .,' for the Scriptures are one form in which the testimony of God is given. The Jews, not having the word of God in their heart, cannot believe the word of God in the Scriptures. ' If you believed Moses, you would believe me, for he wrote about me. If you do not believe his writings, how can you believe my words ? ' Here we have the real ground for the assertion that Moses is the ' accuser ' of the unbelieving Jews. It is not given explicitly in the papyrus.

The third saying occurs in the ' trial scene ' of John ix. Here the blind man whom Jesus had healed is being examined by the Pharisees. He suggests (perhaps ironically) that the reason why they are so anxious to get at the facts is that they wish to become disciples of Jesus (ix. 27). The Pharisees indignantly repudiate the suggestion : they are ' disciples of Moses ' (an expression used in the Talmud of scribes of the Pharisaic school in distinction from the Sadducees and therefore appropriate to the ' Pharisees ' of John rather than to the ' rulers ' of the papyrus, who are distinguished from the ' scribes '). They continue, ' We know that God spoke to Moses, but as for this man, we do not know whence he comes.' This is obviously a logical development of thought. If the Fourth Evangelist took the saying in question from the ' Unknown Gospel ' he certainly showed great skill in fitting it into an entirely different context. If, on the other hand, we suppose that the borrowing was on the other side, we cannot perhaps admire so greatly the skill of our unknown author. Jesus has said, ' Moses, on whom you have set your hope, is your accuser.' The ' rulers ' reply, ' We know that God spoke to Moses, but we do not know whence you come.' In other words, ' You appeal to the authority of Moses ; we accept his authority, but we do not accept yours.' It is no doubt an effective retort in its way, but it is no argument, and no real answer to what Jesus has said.

It would be rash to deny the possibility that the Fourth Evangelist found these sayings in a source represented by our papyrus, and made more effective use of them. But at least it seems clear that they are thoroughly ' at home ' in the contexts where they occur in his work, and in view of the presumption created by our study of the language, it seems best to suppose that the author of the papyrus has excerpted the three sayings from the Fourth Gospel. In this case *Egerton Pap. 2* becomes an early authority for the Western Text of John v. 39, and the only known Greek authority for it. It would, however, be well to postpone a final decision until we have discussed the next episode in the papyrus.

Meanwhile it remains to consider the opening and the close of this section, which are incomplete. At the beginning all that is certain is that Jesus said something ' to the lawyers ', and that what He said contained the words πά]ντα τὸν παραπράσσ[οντα . . .] μον καὶ μὴ ἐμέ. The rather rare verb παραπράσσειν has, according to L. and S., the senses, ' to do a thing beyond or beside the main purpose ', ' to help in doing ', ' to act unjustly ', especially ' to exact money wrongfully '. Of these meanings, only the third seems to give any good sense here. The editors restore πάντα τὸν παραπράσσοντα καὶ ἄνομον, ' every wrongdoer and transgressor '. In view of the uncertainty whether παραπράσσειν was used absolutely except in the sense of ' to exact wrongfully ', I should be inclined to suggest, πάντα τὸν παραπράσσοντα παρὰ νόμον, ' everyone who transgresses against the law ' ; cf. παραβαίνειν παρὰ τήν συγγραφήν cited by L. and S. from an inscription. The whole phrase is in the accusative. The missing word before πάντα was probably a verb. The editors suggest κολάζετε, ' punish '. Another possibility would be the Johannine word ἐλέγχετε, giving the sense ' convict every transgressor against the law, and not me '. Cf. John viii.

46, *Τίς ἐξ ὑμῶν ἐλέγχει με περὶ ἁμαρτίας*, which in any case illustrates the sense.

The sentence which follows was restored by Dr. Kenyon [1] *ὁ γὰρ ἄνομος οὐκ οἶδεν*] *ὃ ποιεῖ πῶς ποιεῖ*, ' The lawless man does not know how he does that which he does ' : cf. John xii. 35, *ὁ περιπατῶν ἐν τῇ σκοτίᾳ οὐκ οἶδεν ποῦ ὑπάγει*. The words *οὐ γὰρ ἔγνωκεν ὃ ποιεῖ πῶς ποιεῖ*, ' for he [*scil.* the transgressor] does not know how he does what he does ', would better fill the space as shown in the transcript. The editors, however, now read the letter before *ο ποιεῖ* as *μ* and the restoration remains uncertain.

The close of the section is missing. The editors restore the last words of Fragment 1, *verso*, *νῦν κατηγορεῖται ὑμῶν ἡ ἀπιστεία* (for *ἀπιστία*). The saying seems to have no canonical parallel, but it may have corresponded in sense to the conclusion of the discourse from which two of the Johannine sayings in this section were taken, John v. 46–47.

SECTION II.   FRAGMENT 1, *recto*, LINES 22–31

The restorations here are only tentative in the opening sentence, but fairly certain for the most part in the succeeding sentences. The text as restored may be rendered as follows :

. . . that they should drag him . . . and, taking up stones together, should stone him.   And the rulers laid hands upon him to seize him and hand him over to the crowd ; and they could not seize him, because the hour of his arrest had not yet come.   But Jesus himself going out from their hands departed from them.

The vocabulary here again is Johannine in character. Of the key-phrases, *λιθάζειν* occurs in no Gospel but the Fourth, in the genuine text of which it occurs 4 times, always with reference to attempts to stone Jesus ; *πιάζειν* occurs in no Gospel but the Fourth, where it occurs 8 times ; two of these are in the Appendix (ch. xxi. 3, 10), with reference to ' catching ' fish, and the other 6 refer to

---

[1] Afterwards Sir Frederick Kenyon.

attempts to arrest Jesus ; the expression ἐληλύθει ἡ ὥρα
is of a form which occurs 14 times in the Fourth Gospel,
once in Matthew and once in Mark ; the verb ἀπονεύειν,
in the sense of ' depart', has its nearest parallel in the
N.T. in the Johannine use of ἐκνεύειν in the same sense
(John v. 13).

In substance also the story recalls the Fourth Gospel.
The Synoptics know of no attempt to stone Jesus. They
all indeed record that after the Cleansing of the Temple
the authorities sought to arrest Jesus, and Luke records
this in terms which partly resemble those of the papyrus :
ἐζήτησαν οἱ γραμματεῖς καὶ οἱ ἀρχιερεῖς ἐπιβαλεῖν ἐπ᾽ αὐτὸν
τὰς χεῖρας ἐν αὐτῇ τῇ ὥρᾳ. Luke again alone records an
attempt made on the life of Jesus at Nazareth (iv. 28–30),
and here the issue is described in terms not unlike those
of the papyrus : αὐτὸς δὲ διελθὼν διὰ μέσου αὐτῶν ἐπορεύετο.

But for really close parallels to the account given in the
papyrus we must turn to the Fourth Gospel. In vii. 30
we read, ' They [indefinite plural] sought to seize (πιάσαι)
him, and no one laid a hand upon him, because his hour
had not yet come.' This attempt having failed, ' the chief
priests and Pharisees sent officers to seize him (ἵνα πιάσωσιν
αὐτόν) ' (32). The crowd is divided in sympathy ; some
are disposed to give consideration to the Messianic claims
of Jesus ; but ' some wished to seize him ; but no one
laid hands upon him ' (44). Consequently the officers
return to their principals without having effected an arrest.
At a later point (viii. 20) the statement is repeated, ' No
one seized him, because his hour had not yet come.' At
the close of the same long section of the Gospel we have
the statement, ' they took up stones to throw at him, but
Jesus concealed himself and went out of the Temple '
(viii. 59). The intention of the evangelist appears to have
been to ' stage ' the great controversial scene at the Feast
of Tabernacles on a background of official and popular
hostility which at any moment might result in the ' seizure '
of Jesus, but which is held at bay by his personal prestige
(vii. 31, 41, 46), until the destined ' hour ' should arrive.

Again, in John x. 31 we read ' The Jews took up stones to stone him.' Jesus protests. They reply, ' It is not for a good deed that we are for stoning you, but for blasphemy ' (33). Jesus again replies, and then, ' they sought to seize him ; and he departed out of their hand ' (39).

The similarity between these passages and the story in the papyrus is obvious. In the fragmentary state of the MS. it is difficult to be quite sure what the exact procedure was ; but so much is clear, that ' rulers ' and the ' crowd ' were concerned in an attempt (*a*) to stone Jesus, and (*b*) to seize him. The attempt is unsuccessful ' because the hour of his arrest had not yet come '. The language all through is Johannine, except that the Johannine phrase οὔπω ἐληλύθει αὐτοῦ ἡ ὥρα is supplemented by the words τῆς παραδόσεως. With this we may compare Mark xiv. 41 : ἦλθεν ἡ ὥρα, ἰδοὺ παραδίδοται ὁ υἱὸς τοῦ ἀνθρώπου.[1]

The question must again be raised whether the Fourth Gospel or the papyrus represents the prior form of the story. Once again we must try to apply the tests of language and of content.

(i) Every stage of the narrative is described in ' Johannine ' phraseology, though the conclusion slightly resembles a passage in Luke.

Papyrus.	Luke.	John.
αὐτὸς δὲ ὁ κύριος	αὐτὸς δὲ	v. 13, ὁ γὰρ Ἰησοῦς ἐξ-
ἐξελθὼν ἐκ τῶν	διελθὼν διὰ	ένευσεν ὄχλου ὄντος
χειρῶν ἀπένευσεν	μέσον αὐτῶν	ἐν τῷ τόπῳ.
ἀπ' αὐτῶν	ἐπορεύετο	viii. 59, Ἰησοῦς δὲ ἐκρύβη καὶ
		ἐξῆλθεν ἐκ τοῦ ἱε-
		ροῦ.

[Johannine words underlined,   xii. 36, ἀπελθὼν ἐκρύβη ἀπ' Lucan words underlined doubly.]   αὐτῶν.

---

[1] The verb παραδιδόναι is used of the procedure which results in the arrest and committal of an offender : cf. Mark i. 14, xiii. 9, 11, Acts iii. 13, viii. 3, etc. It does not in itself mean ' to betray ', though the procedure by which the arrest of Jesus was effected was actually a ' betrayal '.

The coincidence, however, between the language of the papyrus and that of the Fourth Gospel is not so decisive in this case as in the case of Section I, because here the common vocabulary is not so widely distributed through the Gospel. Ἐπιβάλλειν τὰς χεῖρας does not occur in John outside the passage cited. Λιθάζειν occurs only in the passage cited, and in a reference to it in xi. 8. Πιάζειν occurs only once outside the passages cited, except for two occurrences in the Appendix. Only the phrase ἐληλύθει ἡ ὥρα is a constant feature of the Johannine vocabulary. Apart from it, the examination of the language would leave it possible that John was using a source represented by the papyrus. But are we to believe that it was that source that provided him with the conception of the divinely-ordained ' Hour ', which controls the scheme of the Fourth Gospel from its first introduction in ii. 4 to the solemn proclamation in xvii. 1, Πάτερ, ἐλήλυθεν ἡ ὥρα? It is no doubt conceivable that the evangelical tradition evolved the phrase ἡ ὥρα τῆς παραδόσεως αὐτοῦ, on the analogy of the Marcan phrase cited, and that the Fourth Evangelist adapted it to his purpose. But to me it seems more likely that our unknown author took over the phrase from the Fourth Gospel without fully appreciating its import. In John ' the Hour ' is an expression laden with deep theological meaning. It is the appointed ' zero-hour ' of the universe, the hour of the Last Judgment, when the prince of this world is cast out, the moment when the glory of the Lord shall be revealed and all flesh shall see it together (cf. xii. 23–32). To our author the phrase ' his hour ' seemed too vague ; he gave it a more precise but more prosaic meaning as the predestined moment for the arrest of Jesus.

(ii) If we regard the substance of the story, two hypotheses seem possible. (a) The papyrus represents the more primitive tradition of an occasion when Jesus was in danger of being ' lynched ', when ' the rulers ' and ' the crowd ' conspired to seize and stone Him ; and John has for his own purposes made out of this two scenes, in one of which the authorities attempt an arrest, and in the other the populace attempt to stone Him ; the latter being dupli- cated in viii. 59 and x. 31.   (*b*) The author of the ' Un- known Gospel' has conflated two incidents in the Fourth Gospel.   It is unfortunate that the details of the papyrus narrative are obscure through the fragmentary state of the MS. ; but so far as we can gather it appears that the auth- orities attempted to seize Jesus in order to hand Him over to the crowd for stoning.   If, however, the crowd was ready to stone Jesus, surely they did not need to wait for a formal arrest.   In the Fourth Gospel the contemplated arrest is evidently intended to lead to regular legal proceedings, as in fact actually happened in the end (cf. xi. 57, xviii. 2–3, 12).   The Johannine account is more perspicuous and more credible than that of the papyrus, at least so far as we can restore it.   There is indeed a certain amount of repetition or duplication in the Fourth Gospel, which is due to that evangelist's method of composition, but it remains true that his various statements seem to be based upon a tradition of two separate and distinct events rather than upon the account of a single event as we have it in the papyrus.

If now we take together the two ' Johannine ' sections of the papyrus, it seems probable that the author of the ' Unknown Gospel' composed one part of his work by abridging and conflating portions of the Fourth Gospel. In that Gospel he read that before the final crisis the hostility of the Jewish authorities to Jesus had led to an attempt or attempts on His life.   The record of this is in the Fourth Gospel embedded in lengthy theological dis- quisitions, which our author did not wish to reproduce for his readers.   He has selected salient points in the controversy between Jesus and the ' rulers ', as recorded in the Fourth Gospel, and made them lead up to a scene in which two unsuccessful attempts on the life of Jesus, as recorded in the same Gospel, are combined in one episode.   For the most part he has used the very language of the Fourth Gospel, though in the word νομικός, and possibly in the phrase ἡ ὥρα τῆς παραδόσεως he betrays knowledge of non-Johannine forms of the evangelical tradition.

SECTION III.   FRAGMENT 1, *recto*, LINES 32–41

The story of the healing of a leper is apparently all but complete, and the restorations are for the most part fairly certain.   It reads as follows :

And behold a leper approached him and said, ' Rabbi Jesus, when I was travelling with lepers and eating with them at the inn, I became leprous myself also.   If therefore you will, I shall be cleansed.'   Then the Lord said, ' I will : be clean.' And at once the leprosy departed from him.   And the Lord said to him, ' Go and show yourself to the priests.'

This is clearly the same story as that which is given in Mark i. 40–44, and the Synoptic parallels.   A leper approached Jesus saying, ' If you will, I am cleansed ' (' you can cleanse me,' Synn.).   Jesus said, ' I will ; be clean . . . show yourself to the priest(s).'   Such is the nucleus of the story in all our sources alike.   But apart from the words of Jesus and of the leper, there is little directly in common between the Synoptics and the ' Unknown Gospel '.   Nor does the language of the papyrus show decisive affinity with one Synoptic Gospel more than another, as the following analysis will show :

Papyrus.

Papyrus	
καὶ	all three Synoptics.
ἰδού	Matthew and Luke.
λεπρὸς	Matthew and Mark.
προσελθὼν	Matthew only.
αὐτῷ	Matthew only, πρὸς αὐτόν, Mark.
λέγει	λέγων, all three.
ἐὰν σὺ θέλῃς	ἐὰν θέλῃς, all three.
καθαρίζομαι	δύνασαί με καθαρίσαι, all three.
θέλω, καθαρίσθητι	all three.

ἀπέστη απ᾿ αὐτοῦ ἡ λέπρα   ἀπῆλθεν ἀπ᾿ αὐτοῦ ἡ λέπρα, Mark.
                              ἡ λέπρα ἀπῆλθεν ἀπ᾿ αὐτοῦ, Luke.
πορευθεὶς ἐπίδειξον   ⎫   ὕπαγε σεαυτὸν δεῖξον τῷ ερεῖ,
                  ⎬(?) Matthew, Mark.
σεαυτὸν τοῖς ἱερεῦσιν ⎭   ἀπελθὼν δεῖξον σεαυτὸν τῶ ἱερεῖ,
                              Luke.
                              (Cf. πορευθέντες ἐπιδείξατε ἑαυ-
τοὺς τοῖς ἱερεῦσιν, Luke xvii. 14.)

If we are to take the view that the author of the ' Un-known Gospel ' derived the story from a canonical source, we should have to suppose that he knew all three Synoptic Gospels, and produced his account by combining expressions used by different evangelists. Possible, no doubt ; but is it likely ?

But further, there are certain characteristic traits which are present in all three Synoptics, and are lacking in the papyrus : (a) the leper did obeisance to Jesus (γονυπετῶν, Mark, προσεκύνει, Matthew, πεσὼν ἐπὶ πρόσωπον, Luke) ; (b) Jesus stretched out His hand and touched him ; (c) Jesus charged him to tell no one. Mark also adds that Jesus was either sorry for the man (σπλαγχνισθείς, most MSS.), or angry with him (ὀργισθείς, Codex Bezæ, and some Old Latin and Syriac MSS.) ; and that when He sent him away He was indignant (ἐμβριμησάμενος). It is an odd thing that two of the expressions here missing in the papyrus appear in later sections, ἐμβριμησάμενος in Section IV, ἐκτείνας τὴν χεῖρα in Section V. Is this a mere accident, or does it suggest that the author's mind unconsciously retained a memory of what he had just read in Mark, and although he did not use it immediately, introduced it into different contexts ? It may be so. But if we suppose that the author had thus before him the Synoptic account, we are put to it to understand why he should have left out these highly characteristic traits of the story, unless he was sorely pressed for space. This, however, he was not, for he has expanded the story by a quite unparalleled addition. The leper said, ' As I was travelling

in the company of lepers, and eating with them in the inn,
I contracted leprosy myself'. The intention is apparently
to enlist the sympathy of Jesus with a person who had had
such bad luck as to contract a loathsome disease while
travelling on his lawful occasions. The spirit of this *ad
misericordiam* appeal reminds one of the version of the story
of the man with a withered hand in the Gospel according
to the Hebrews, where the man says, ' I was a bricklayer,
earning my living with my hands. I beg you, Jesus,
restore to me my health, that I may not be disgraced by
begging for food.' Is this mere embroidery of a narrative
taken by the author of the apocryphal Gospel from one
of the Synoptic Gospels, or was he following a different
oral tradition ? We cannot answer the question, because
only this part of the apocryphal version is preserved. It
is usually said, chiefly on the basis of certain not too clear
statements in the Fathers, that the Gospel according to the
Hebrews had some special relation to the Gospel according
to Matthew. But among the fragments preserved there
are at least 10 which have no obvious parallel in Matthew
or the other Synoptic Gospels. It is perfectly possible that
the source, written or (more probably) oral, from which
these passages were drawn, contained also alternative
versions of such stories as those of the Withered Hand, the
Talents, and the Rich Ruler, all of which show striking
differences from the canonical forms.

There is the same doubt about the story of the leper in
the ' Unknown Gospel'. At a former stage of Gospel
criticism emphasis was laid so exclusively upon literary
source-criticism that all variations tended to be explained
as editorial rehandling of written sources. The emergence
of ' form-criticism ' has drawn attention afresh to the fact
that, whatever the literary history of the tradition may
have been, it had a previous history in an oral form, and
that variations must have arisen at this stage, before written
sources existed. It would therefore be unwise to assume
that the resemblances between the leper-story in the
papyrus and in the canonical Gospels are due to the use

of the latter by the author of the former. The resemblances are after all confined to that minimum which could not be absent if the story was to be told at all. The differences, both by way of omission and of addition, are more striking. It may well be that the story had taken different forms in the oral tradition, and that it reached the author of the ' Unknown Gospel ' in a form different from that which it took in the tradition underlying Mark, which is itself the basis of all the canonical reports.

Section IV. Fragment 2, *recto*, lines 43–59

The second fragment is more incomplete than the first, and a good deal of restoration is necessary ; but the restorations proposed by the editors in the *recto* text seem in the main inevitable. The text as restored may be translated as follows :

. . . came to him and tested him by examination, saying, Rabbi Jesus, we know that you have come from God ; for the things you are doing bear witness beyond all the prophets. Tell us then, is it lawful to pay to kings (or, to the Emperors) those things which pertain to the Government ? Shall we pay or shall we not ? And Jesus, knowing their mind (?), indignantly said to them, Why do you call me Rabbi, when you do not listen to what I say ? Finely did Isaiah prophesy concerning you, saying, This people honour me with their lips, but their heart is far from me. In vain do they worship me . . . commandments. . . .

It seems clear that we have a narrative parallel to the Synoptic story of the Tribute Money (Mark xii. 13–17 and parallels). The main structure of the story can be recognized.

1. Jesus is put to the test ($\pi\varepsilon\iota\varrho\acute{\alpha}\zeta\varepsilon\iota\nu$) with a question.
2. The question is introduced by a flattering remark.
3. The question is put in a double form : ' Is it lawful . . .? '—' Shall we pay or not ? '
4. Jesus recognizes the intention of the questioners.
5. He replies with a reproachful question : ' Why do

you call me Rabbi' (papyrus), or ' Why do you test me ? ' (Synn.).

But while the general form of the passage is closely similar to the Synoptic narrative, nothing but the barest minimum of words is common to the canonical Gospels and the papyrus :

ἐπείραζον	cf. τί με πειράζετε, Matthew, Mark, not Luke.
διδάσκαλε	all three.
οἴδαμεν ὅτι	all three.
γὰρ	Matthew, Mark.
εἰπέ οὖν ἡμῖν (?)	εἰπὸν οὖν ἡμῖν, Matthew only.
ἐξὸν	ἔξεστιν, all three.
ἀποδοῦναι	δοῦναι, all three.
ἀποδῶμεν αὐτοῖς ἢ μή	δῶμεν ἢ μὴ δῶμεν, Mark only.
ὁ δὲ Ἰησοῦς εἰδὼς,	γνοὺς δὲ ὁ Ἰησοῦς, Matthew.
τὴν διάνοιαν αὐτῶν (?)	τὴν πονηρίαν αὐτῶν, Matthew.
	αὐτῶν τὴν ὑπόκρισιν, Matthew.
	αὐτῶν τὴν πανουργίαν, Luke.
εἶπεν αὐτοῖς,	Mark.
τί με.	Matthew, Mark.

There is here certainly no amount of resemblance in language sufficient to justify the hypothesis that the ' Unknown Gospel' is directly dependent on any of the Synoptic Gospels. That hypothesis becomes still more unlikely in view of the striking divergences from the Synoptic account.

(i) The flattering remark which introduces the question has the form, οἴδαμεν ὅτι ἀπὸ θεοῦ ἐλήλυθας, ἃ γὰρ ποιεῖς μαρτυρεῖ παρὰ τοὺς προφήτας πάντας. This is thoroughly ' Johannine ' in character. The idea that the works of Jesus ' bear witness' to Him is familiar in the Fourth Gospel ; and cf. John iii. 2, where Nicodemus says, ῾Ραββεῖ, οἴδαμεν ὅτι ἀπὸ θεοῦ ἐλήλυθας διδάσκαλος οὐδεὶς γὰρ δύναται ταῦτα τὰ σημεῖα ποιεῖν ἃ σὺ ποιεῖς ἐὰν μὴ ᾖ ὁ θεὸς μετ' αὐτοῦ. In view of the relation we have seen to exist between the

'Unknown Gospel' and the Gospel according to John, we need not hesitate to assume a reminiscence of this passage.

(ii) Instead of the definite 'tribute to Cæsar' we have the vaguer 'things-pertaining-to-the-Government to kings' —τοῖς βασιλεῦσιν, which might indeed mean 'to the emperors,' βασιλεύς being the ordinary title of the Emperor in the East. But cf. Matt. xvii. 25, οἱ βασιλεῖς τῆς γῆς ἀπὸ τινῶν λαμβάνουσι τέλη. This is another question relating to the payment of taxes, and the vaguer form of phrase is used, as in the papyrus.

(iii) Τί με καλεῖτε τῷ στόματι ὑμῶν διδάσκαλον μὴ ἀκούοντες ὃ λέγω ; Cf. Luke vi. 46, Τί με καλεῖτε Κύριε, κύριε, καὶ οὐ ποιεῖτε ἃ λέγω ; The most probable account of the matter is that this saying circulated in oral tradition in isolation. The compiler of 'Q' supplied it with the context in which it stands in Luke ; the author of the 'Unknown Gospel,' or his immediate authority, gave it a different context.

(iv) Καλῶς Ἡσαΐας περὶ ὑμῶν ἐπροφήτευσεν εἰπών . . . Cf. Matt. xv. 7, καλῶς ἐπροφήτευσεν περὶ ὑμῶν Ἡσαΐας, λέγων, introducing the same quotation from Isa. xxix. 13. The context is entirely different, but it looks as if the author had taken the quotation, with its proper introduction, from Matthew (who follows Mark, but with modifications which bring the passage nearer to the form in the papyrus), and supplied it with a different context. But this inference is not certain, for (a) this method of introduction is not peculiar to that passage ; cf. Acts xxviii. 25, καλῶς τὸ πνεῦμα τὸ ἅγιον ἐλάλησεν διὰ Ἡσαΐου. It may therefore have been a customary way of citing prophecy. (b) The quotation does not exactly follow the form given in Matthew and Mark, but is generally near to the LXX form.

LXX.	Papyrus.	Matthew–Mark
ὁ λαὸς οὗτος	ὁ λαὸς οὗτος	οὗτος ὁ λαὸς
ἐν τοῖς χείλεσιν αὐτῶν	τοῖς χείλεσιν αὐτῶν	τοῖς χείλεσιν

τιμῶσίν με	τιμῶσίν με	με τιμᾷ
ματὴν δὲ σέβονταί με	ματήν με σέβονται	ματὴν δὲ σέβονταί με
διδάσκοντες ἐντάλματα ἀνθρώπων καὶ διδασκαλίας.	ἐντάλματα [ἀνθρώπων διδάσκοντες] (?)	διδάσκοντες διδασκαλίας ἐντάλματα ἀνθρώπων.

Moreover the words τῷ στόματι ὑμῶν in the preceding clause are clearly a reminiscence of the words of the preceding clause in the LXX, ἐγγίζει μοι ὁ λαὸς οὗτος ἐν τῷ στόματι αὐτῶν. It is clear, therefore, that if the author did get the quotation from Matthew, he has verified it for himself from the LXX text. It is perhaps simpler to suppose that he took the quotation either directly from the LXX, or from some collection of *testimonia*, independently of the canonical Gospels.

The case therefore for regarding this passage as based upon the canonical Gospels is far from strong. We have indeed probably an instructive instance of the way in which the tradition shaped itself in the course of transmission. We may suppose that in the early oral tradition there was a story of a question about payment of taxes, which took two forms, one a more vague and general one which spoke of ' kings ' and of ' things pertaining to the Government ' the other a more definite one which spoke of ' Cæsar ' and ' tribute '. In both forms the question was regarded as an attempt to put Jesus to the test (πειράζειν). In both cases the question was prefaced by a flattering remark, which Jesus deprecates. The form of the remark and of Jesus' reply may well have differed in different forms of the story. The tradition knew of other cases in which Jesus was addressed in flattering terms, which He brushed aside, e.g. Mark x. 17–18 : ' Good Master . . . '—' Why call me good ? ' ; John iii. 2. In the form of tradition known to our author the reply of Jesus was probably already given in the form of the floating saying utilized otherwise in Luke vi. 46, and he may himself have given to the introductory remark a form due to his knowledge of John iii. 2

He (or his immediate authority) has further supplemented the saying of Jesus with a quotation from the O.T., as the canonical evangelists have done in several places. The actual reply of Jesus to the question asked is unfortunately not preserved in the papyrus.

We conclude therefore that in this part of the ' Unknown Gospel ' the author is probably dependent, directly or indirectly, on an oral tradition different from that which underlies the parallel passage in the Synoptic Gospels. The mould in which the story is cast is manifestly the same, but the actual wording is almost entirely different. This is exactly the state of affairs we should expect to find if the variations took place in the pre-literary stage. The relation of this passage to the Synoptic parallel is probably similar to that which exists between the story of the Centurion's Servant in Matthew and Luke, and the story of the Nobleman's Son in John. We can hardly doubt that it is the same story, yet the wide difference in the actual wording makes any literary dependence unlikely.

SECTION V.   FRAGMENT 2, *verso*, LINES 60–75

The text here is woefully fragmentary, and restoration is problematical. We shall do well to start from those phrases which are clear beyond reasonable doubt.

The first 3 lines are very obscure. Then we have the clear statement that certain persons ' were at a loss about the strange question ' which Jesus had asked. Presumably we are to look for this strange question in the fragmentary words in lines 60–62. Thereupon, ' Jesus, as he walked, stood upon the verge of the River Jordan and stretching out his right hand . . . ' did something which is no longer clear. The next words which can be read are καὶ κατέσπειρεν ἐπὶ τὸν . . . Κατασπείρειν means ' to sow ', ' scatter ', ' sprinkle '. Two lines further down we read ὕδωρ, ' water ', and again two lines further, ' brought forth fruit '. Those are the last intelligible words.

What are we to make of this? There is no passage in the canonical Gospels which seems to give any help. Since

early in the passage we have a reference to ' sowing ' (or
' scattering'), and later the expression ' brought forth
fruit ', it would seem natural to suppose that we have a
story in which Jesus sowed seed which forthwith sprang up
and bore fruit. On this supposition we might restore lines
68–69 ἐκτείνα[ς τὴν] χεῖ[ρα αὐτο]ῦ τὴν δεξιὰν [ἐγέ]μισεν
[σπόρῳ κ]αὶ κατέσπειρ[εν ἐπ]ὶ τὸν. . . ον, 'He stretched
out his right hand and filled it with seed, and sowed it
upon the . . . ' : upon what? The editors suggest the
river, restoring ποταμόν at the beginning of line 70. But
in lines 70–71 we have fragments of words which can hardly
be restored otherwise than as κατε[σπαρμ]ένον ὕδωρ. If the
suggested interpretation we are following is to be accepted,
then these words must mean ' the water which had been
sowed with seed ', and this, as the editors say, though perhaps just possible, is all but incredible as a rendering of
the Greek. Κατεσπαρμένον ὕδωρ could in fact hardly mean
anything but ' sprinkled water '. It appears therefore that
what Jesus ' sowed ', or ' sprinkled ' was not seed but
water. In that case He must have sprinkled it not ' upon
the river ', but ' upon the shore '. I suggest therefore
αἰγιαλόν instead of ποταμόν at the beginning of line 70.
Αἰγιαλός indeed is properly the sea-shore ; but in Egyptian
papyri it is used of the shores of the marshy lakes which
are found in Lower Egypt (see Moulton and Milligan,
Vocabulary, s.v.). Our papyrus is also Egyptian, and it
seems not impossible that the word should here be used
for the shore of a river.

With this clue I propose, tentatively, to restore the
passage as follows :

[π]εριπατῶν ὁ Ἰησοῦς [ἐ]στάθη
[ἐπὶ τοῦ] χείλους τοῦ Ἰο[ρδ]άνου
[ποταμ]οῦ, καὶ ἐκτείνα[ς τὴν] χεῖ-
[ρα αὐτο]ῦ τὴν δεξιὰν [ἐγέ]μισεν
[ὕδατι κ]αὶ κατέσπειρ[εν ἐπ]ὶ τὸν
[αἰγιαλ]όν · καὶ τότε [δὴ τὸ] κατε-
[σπαρμ]ένον ὕδωρ ἔ[νυγρο]ν τὴν

D

[γῆν ἐποίησε] καὶ ἐπ[οτίσ]θη [1] ἐνώ-
[πιον αὐτῶν, ἐ]ξήγα[γ]εν δὲ καρπόν.

Jesus, as he walked, stood still upon the verge of the River Jordan ; and stretching out his right hand, he filled it with water and sprinkled it upon the shore ; and thereupon the sprinkled water made the ground moist, and it was watered before them and brought forth fruit.

It is a bizarre story, implying a nature-miracle unknown to the other Gospels, canonical and apocryphal alike. The motive underlying it seems to be the popular belief in the fecundating power of water, which is widespread, and was particularly strong in Egypt, where the pheno-menon of fertilization by Nile-water seemed a yearly miracle. The story, in fact, has something of the character of a folk-tale. We must, however, recognize that folk-tale motives have at times entered even into the canonical Gospels, to say nothing of the apocryphal. The stories of the Coin in the Fish's Mouth, the Blasted Fig-tree, and the Turning of Water into Wine can all be paralleled out of folk-lore. In the Gospels the last certainly, the second probably, and the first possibly, have a certain symbolic intention, and we may assume that some such intention was present in the ' Unknown Gospel ', since the act is performed by Jesus to illustrate a ' strange question ' which He had propounded. In view of the Johannine affinities of this document, we should probably look to the Fourth Gospel for a clue to the symbolism. The symbol of ' living water ' is among its most characteristic ideas. Water stands for the life-giving energies of God. This symbolism is deeply rooted in the Old Testament. Cf. Isa. lv. 10–11 :

For as the rain cometh down and the snow from heaven, and returneth not thither, but watereth the earth, and maketh it bring forth and bud, and giveth seed to the sower and

[1] Εποτίσθη is somewhat long for the presumed lacuna. The editors suggest ἐπλήσθη ' was impregnated ', but without any confidence. A pos-sible restoration would be ἐπ[λησ]θη ἐνω[ρίστερον], ' it was very soon fecun-dated '. The word ἐνωρίστερον is cited from Phylarchus (iii. B.C.). See L. and S.

bread to the eater, so shall my word be that goeth out of my mouth.

The word of the Lord is like water that fertilizes the ground. The symbolic act described in the papyrus may have been conceived as an illustration of this truth. It seems possible to restore the first three lines of the fragment so as to give a question to which the symbolic act might provide the answer. Following some suggestions of the editors I propose (*exempli gratia*) some such restoration as the following :

> [μικρὸν σπέρμα γεωργοῦ]
> [ἐν κρυπ]τῷ τόπῳ [κ]ατακλείσαν-
> [τος, ὡς] [1] ὑποτέτακτα[ι] ἀδήλως,
> [πῶς γίν]εται τὸ βάρος αὐτοῦ ἄστατον ;

When a husbandman has enclosed a small seed in a secret place, so that it is invisibly buried, how does its abundance become immeasurable ?

If something like this was the purport of the question, we may understand the episode on these lines. Jesus makes use of the figure of seed and harvest (which we know to have been a favourite illustration with Him). The seed, He says, is a small thing (cf. Mark iv. 31), and it is buried out of sight (cf. John xii. 24). What causes it to produce an abundant crop ? The answer is, The rain cometh down from heaven and watereth the earth and maketh it bring forth. But instead of giving the answer in words, Jesus takes water and sprinkles it on the earth—and the miracle of fertilization takes place. Even so, it is implied, the word, or the Spirit, of God, like living water, quickens the heart of man.

Whether or not this was the general drift of the passage, one thing is clear. It rests on no source known to us from other Gospel literature. This fact shows that the author, whether or not he was acquainted with our Gospels, had other sources at his command, and makes it the more credible that the unfamiliar forms of the stories of the

---

[1] For ὥστε.

Leper and the Tribute-money were also drawn from sources peculiar to him.

SECTION VI.   FRAGMENT 3, *recto*

The *verso* of Fragment 3, which, according to the editors, came first, defies restoration.   Single words can be read, but it would be hazardous to attempt to make sense of them.   The *recto* is read as follows :

$$
\begin{array}{ll}
\tilde{\varepsilon}\nu\ \dot{\varepsilon}\sigma\mu[\varepsilon\nu & \quad\quad] \\
\mu\acute{\varepsilon}\nu\omega\ \pi[& \lambda\iota] \\
\theta o\upsilon\varsigma\ \varepsilon\dot{\iota}\varsigma\ [& \dot{\alpha}\pi o\text{-}] \\
\varkappa\tau\varepsilon\acute{\iota}\nu\omega[\sigma\iota\nu\ \alpha\dot{\upsilon}\tau\acute{o}\nu &] \\
\lambda\acute{\varepsilon}\gamma\varepsilon\iota\ .\ o[&] \\
[.]\varepsilon[.\ .]\ .\ .\ [&]
\end{array}
$$

There is not much here to guide us ; but cf. John x. 30–31, ἐγὼ καὶ ὁ πατήρ μου ἕν ἐσμεν. ἐβάστασαν πάλιν λίθους οἱ Ἰουδαῖοι ἵνα λιθάσωσιν αὐτόν. ἀπεκρίθη αὐτοῖς ὁ Ἰησοῦς . . ., '. . . I and my Father are one.   The Jews took up stones again to stone him.   Jesus answered them . . .'.   We seem driven to suspect that the papyrus contained something similar to the Johannine passage : ' [Jesus said, I and my Father] are one . . . [They took up] stones . . . to kill him . . . he said . . .'. .

The results may be summarized as follows :

Sections I and II, which probably formed a single *pericope*, are directly based on the Fourth Gospel, containing (*a*) a discourse which is a cento of Johannine passages, and (*b*) a story which seems to be a conflation of two separate incidents in John.   But it also contained a saying addressed to ' lawyers ' with no canonical parallel, and the concluding saying, of which only 5 words survive in part, seems also to be different from anything in the canonical Gospels.

Section III contains a story closely parallel to one in the Synoptics, which may have been derived directly from them, but was more probably taken from a parallel tradition.

Section IV contains a story parallel to one in the Synoptics, but told so differently that we seem driven to postulate an independent tradition. Johannine influence, however, again seems probable.

Section V contains material without any parallel in the canonical Gospels, and clearly points to a different strain of tradition.

Section VI, so far as it can be restored, suggests a Johannine source or parallel.

If the above analysis is right, the only canonical Gospel with which the papyrus text shows any clear and direct relation is the Fourth Gospel. The author *may* have known the Synoptics, and his language *may* have been to some extent influenced by them, but there is no clear evidence of this. The ' Unknown Gospel ' therefore would seem to have emanated from a circle which held the Fourth Gospel to be authoritative, but which, if it knew the Synoptic Gospels, preferred, at least in some cases, other authorities.

On the relation between the papyrus text and non-canonical texts having more or less the character of Gospels, I have little to add to what the editors have said, but a brief summary may be useful.

1. Fragments of Known Apocryphal Gospels

The Gospel according to the Hebrews has, as we have seen, an addition to the story of the Withered Hand which is similar in spirit to the addition to the story of the Leper in the papyrus. We may add that the comparison of Jesus with the prophets (in Section IV) is also in the spirit of the Gospel according to the Hebrews. Note the following passages :

In the story of the Baptism of Jesus, the divine voice says, ' My Son, in all the prophets I awaited thee, that thou mightest come, and that I might find my rest in thee.'

'Even in the prophets, after they were anointed with Holy Spirit, there was found matter of sin' (*sermo peccati*).

To the rich man who asks, 'By doing what good thing shall I live?' Jesus replies, 'Man, do the law *and the prophets*.'

As regards language, the Gospel according to the Hebrews, like the papyrus, refers to Jesus as 'the Lord,' and addresses Him either as '*Jesu*' or as '*magister*' (= διδάσκαλε), but not '*magister Jesu*'; and the formula στραφείς occurs both in the papyrus and in the Gospel according to the Hebrews ('*conversus*').

There is nothing here to suggest that the 'Unknown Gospel' depended on the Gospel according to the Hebrews as a source, but it may well be that the type of tradition followed by the author of the new document had some contact with the tradition underlying that Gospel.

The Ebionite Gospel and the Gospel according to the Egyptians have no resemblance to our document in matter or in style, if we except the single idiom, ἦλθον with the infinitive to express the purpose of the Incarnation : *Egerton Papyrus 2*, ἦλθον κατηγορῆσαι, cf. *Eb.* ἦλθον καταλῦσαι τὰς θυσίας, *Eg.* ἦλθον καταλῦσαι τὰ ἔργα τῆς θηλείας. This, however, is, as I have suggested, of the nature of a formula common to various types of early Christian tradition.

The Gospel according to Peter, so far as it is preserved, contains a Passion-narrative which depends on all four canonical Gospels, and probably not on any independent tradition. In style and language it has nothing in common with our document, unless we include the reference to Jesus as 'the Lord'. This is invariable throughout the extant fragment of the Gospel. In our document, as in Luke and John, it alternates with the more primitive form of reference to Jesus by name.

None of the other apocryphal Gospels known to us by name show any kind of affinity with our document, so far as can be judged from the exiguous fragments preserved.

2. FRAGMENTS OF UNIDENTIFIED DOCUMENTS

Two sets of Sayings of Jesus found at Oxyrhynchus (*Ox. Pap. 1*, 654) may belong to a single document. It was different in character from the ' Unknown Gospel ', consisting entirely of a collection of aphorisms. Consequently there is no sufficient basis for comparison, for our papyrus is lacking in sayings of this aphoristic character. Like our papyrus, however, the Oxyrhynchus Sayings present material parallel to passages in the Synoptic Gospels, but sometimes with variations which suggest a different line of tradition, and also material with no canonical parallel. They also show a certain ' Johannine ' colouring, but nothing like the pronounced Johannine character of Sections I and II of our papyrus. In view of the slight possible contact between our document and the Gospel according to the Hebrews, it is interesting to observe that one of the Oxyrhynchus Sayings is also cited from that Gospel.

Oxyrhynchus Papyrus 655 seems not to be part of the same collection of Sayings, since it lacks the formula λέγει 'Ιησοῦς, though otherwise it is similar in character. It contains part of a conversation of Jesus with His disciples, introducing three sayings parallel, though with variations, to Synoptic sayings, and one which has no close parallel anywhere, but is partly similar to a fragment of the Gospel according to the Egyptians, and partly similar to a saying cited in II Clement.[1]

Ox. Pap. 655 has no point of contact with our document. A papyrus-fragment from the Fayyum in the Rainer collection reads as follows :

[πρὸ δὲ τοῦ μεταλ
λαγεῖν · ὡσαύτως · πάν[τες ἐν ταύτῃ
τῇ νυκτὶ σκανδαλισ [θήσεσθε κατὰ
τὸ γραφέν · πατάξω τὸν [ποιμένα καὶ τὰ

---

[1] On the relation of these three sayings, see Evelyn White, *Sayings of Jesus*, pp. xliv–xlvi.

πρόβατα διασκορπισθήσ[ονται. εἰπόντος
τ]οῦ Πετ · καὶ εἰ πάντες ο[ὐκ ἐγώ, ἔτι αὐτῷ,
ὁ ἀλεκτρύων δὶς κοκ[κύξει, καὶ σὺ
πρῶτον τρὶς ἀ[παρνήσῃ με.

Before parting from them (he said) in like manner, All you
will be scandalised to-night according to that which is written :
' I will smite the shepherd and the sheep will be scattered.'
When Peter said, Even if all, yet not I, (he said) to him
again, The cock will crow twice and you will first deny
me thrice.

The rapid dialogue recalls slightly the manner of Section I
of our papyrus.   Cf. especially εἰπόντος τοῦ Πέτ(ρου) with
αὐτῶν δὲ λεγόντων.   But the staccato, almost ' telegraphic '
style of the Fayyum papyrus goes far beyond the concise
brevity of our document.   The Fayyum fragment may be
simply a sort of ' précis ' of Mark xiv. 27–30, Matt. xxvi.
31–34 (following partly Mark and partly Matthew).

Ox. Pap. 840 contains a long and circumstantial account
of a controversy between Jesus and a Chief Priest, having
no parallel in the canonical Gospels.   It is probably an
extract from an apocryphal Gospel.   The style has no
resemblance to that of *Eg. Pap. 2*, nor is there any common
character in the vocabulary.   Jesus is referred to throughout as ὁ σωτήρ.   Grenfell and Hunt held that the document
of which *Ox. Pap. 840* is a fragment was composed about
A.D. 200.

The only relevant inference that we can draw from the
examination of these anonymous fragments is that the
Church in Egypt had in early times a considerable supply
of extra-canonical Gospel tradition which was incorporated
in various documents, and that such apocryphal documents
found a ready public in that country.   The newly-published fragment adds to the number of works of this kind.
It cannot with any probability be associated with any as
the fragments previously known, as part of the same work.
As the number of apocryphal Gospel documents increases,
it becomes less and less plausible to suppose that they all

originated in expansions of material derived from the canonical Gospels, assumed to be already familiar in Egypt.

It follows from the above discussion that the importance of the newly-published papyrus lies chiefly in two directions:

(i) More perhaps than any apocryphal Gospel text yet known, with the possible exception of the Gospel according to the Hebrews, it provides material for the study of variant forms of evangelical tradition.

(ii) It affords what is probably the earliest actual quotation from the Fourth Gospel. Assuming that the papyrus was written about A.D. 150, it would be reasonable to place the composition of the ' Unknown Gospel ' of which it is a copy substantially earlier. The editors believe that ' it was of comparative early date, most likely before the end of the first century '.[1] I should myself not care to put it quite so far back, but a date early in the second century is likely. Now there is no certain citation of the Fourth Gospel in Ignatius (probably A.D. 115), or in Papias (usually dated about 140, but perhaps earlier), or in Polycarp (usually dated about 115, but perhaps later). It is highly probable that the Gospel was used by Valentinus and Basilides (about 130), but it is not certain that the citations we possess are from the works of these teachers themselves rather than from works of their followers. Thus our previously extant literature contains no undoubted quotation from the Fourth Gospel earlier than Justin, Tatian and the Gospel according to Peter, all of which belong to the middle years of the second century. The composition of the ' Unknown Gospel ' is almost certainly to be dated earlier than this.

It has indeed been doubted by many critics whether the

---

[1] A date as early as this is necessary if it be held that the Fourth Evangelist used our document as a source, but not if a common source was used by both authors, still less if it be held (as I have argued) that the papyrus depends upon the Fourth Gospel.

Gospel according to John was actually published before about A.D. 135. But as it happens, we are now in a position to say with some definiteness that it was known in Egypt about as early as this. A papyrus in the Rylands Library, Manchester, has recently been published, containing parts of John xviii. 31–33, 37–38. See *An Unpublished Fragment of the Fourth Gospel*, by C. H. Roberts, Manchester University Press, 1935. The editor of the Rylands papyrus dates it to the first half of the second century, and is able to claim the support of other experts for this dating. Its style of writing resembles that of *Eg. Pap. 2*, but it appears to be, if anything, somewhat earlier. We shall not be far wrong therefore if we say that the Rylands MS. of the Fourth Gospel was written not later than A.D. 140. If so, it is the earliest piece of Christian writing known. It was presumably written in Egypt. The Fourth Gospel was almost certainly published at Ephesus, and, allowing time for it to reach Egypt under the conditions of book-circulation in the ancient world, we may fairly conclude that the date of composition was not later than A.D. 120. That being so, we have an additional argument against the view that the ' Unknown Gospel ' was used by the Fourth Evangelist as a source, though of course it does not tell against the view that John and the author of the ' Unknown Gospel ' used a common source. But if the arguments I have put forth are held to make it probable that the ' Unknown Gospel ' borrows from the Fourth Gospel, then we may put together the evidence of *Eg. Pap. 2* and *Ryl. Pap. Gk. 457*, and say that they prove not only that the Fourth Gospel circulated in Egypt during the first half of the second century, but also that it was sufficiently well-known and respected to be used in the composition of another Gospel-writing quite early in that century. In that case we should be compelled to push back our provisional terminus *ad quem* for the composition of John, some twenty years earlier, to about the beginning of the century.

This leads to some reflections upon the reception of the Gospels in the Egyptian Church. *Eg. Pap. 2*, as we have seen, affords no convincing evidence of the use of the Synoptic Gospels, for although two of the stories in it have parallels in the Synoptics, the variations are so great that it is easier to suppose that a different tradition is being followed. Now it may be an accident, but it is a fact that there is no actual evidence of the reception of the Synoptic Gospels in Egypt as early as this. On the other hand, there is evidence that the Egyptians were addicted to Gospel-writings of an ' apocrychal ' character. Not only was there a ' Gospel according to the Egyptians,' but the Oxyrhynchus Papyri have yielded at least one, and probably two, collections of Sayings of Jesus, and a fragment (840) which seems to have belonged to some kind of Gospel, and to these we must add the Fayyum fragment and now *Eg. Pap. 2.* It is thought by some that the Gospel according to Peter was composed in Egypt. This I think improbable, but at least it was in Egypt that the extant fragment was discovered, attesting the circulation of the work in that country. This evidence is, of course, not all early, and we must always allow for the fact that Egypt is the only country where papyri have been preserved to any extent. But it is noteworthy that Clement of Alexandria, though he accepts the four-Gospel canon, cites the Gospel according to the Egyptians with a respect which has often been thought somewhat surprising.

The evidence suggests, though it is far from proving, that before the middle of the second century the Synoptic Gospels had not yet secured any exclusive authority in Egypt. They may have been known, but traditions independent of them were sometimes preferred, and Gospels circulated which were based on these alternative traditions. The Fourth Gospel, on the other hand, would seem to have leapt into favour almost as soon as it appeared.[1] The

---

[1] If it should seem likely on a balance of arguments that Section III was based upon the Synoptic record (for Section IV this seems to me too improbable to be considered seriously), it would still remain true that the author of the Unknown Gospel treated the Fourth Gospel with greater respect than the Synoptics, since he follows its exact wording, while he alters them freely.

Rylands Papyrus, the Egerton Papyrus, Basilides, Valentinus,[1] Theodotus the Valentinian,[2] provide a continuous series of testimonies beginning perhaps as early as 120, and going on to the middle years of the second century. During this period we have some evidence that Valentinus, and the Basilidians, used Matthew and Luke, but these Gospels clearly do not possess for them the same importance as John. Towards the close of the century we reach Clement of Alexandria, and although he accepts the Synoptic Gospels as authoritative, it is clear that for him, as for Origen and their successors in the school of Alexandria, the Fourth Gospel is pre-eminent. There was evidently in that Gospel something that specially appealed to the Egyptian mind.

The earliest history of Christianity in Egypt is strangely obscure. It may be that these new discoveries throw some little light upon it.

---

[1] Valentinus came to Rome about 135, but he had previously preached in Egypt, where his school flourished.

[2] Excerpted by Clement, probably an Alexandrian follower of Valentinus.

3. MATTHEW AND PAUL

(1947)

'MATTHEW', says Papias, 'composed the Logia in the Hebrew language.' Some moderns have surmised that he is alluding to a document now lost, which may have served as a source to the First Evangelist. The ancient Church did not so understand him. 'Matthew,' says Irenæus, 'among the Hebrews, in their own language, brought out a written Gospel (γραφὴν εὐαγγελίου).' From that time it has been a fixed point in the tradition that our First Gospel in comparison with the others has in some special sense a Jewish character. As a rough generalization it will serve, though not without qualifications which I need not detail. It is at least apparent that those scholars who in recent years have so greatly enriched our understanding of the Jewish background of the Gospels generally find this Gospel exceptionally apt to their purpose. Modern critics, who recognize diverse sources behind our canonical Matthew, have pointed out that in certain portions of the Gospel we seem to find a more emphatic Jewish colouring than in others ; and not only a Jewish colouring, but even a certain anti-Gentile bias, and along with it an antagonism to Paul, the Apostle of the Gentiles.

This anti-Pauline bias, if such it is, is not to be equally recognized in all parts of the Gospel. The judgment of the old Tübingen school provides a formula which accounts for many of the facts : that the Gospel according to Matthew represents a first approach from the Jewish-Christian side to the Catholicism which was to provide the Hegelian synthesis between the primitive Judaic Christianity in which that Gospel is rooted and the Gentile Christianity of Paul. In any case, the presumed sources of this Gospel and the process of its composition, so far as criticism is able to reconstruct it, would seem to belong

53

to a *milieu* remote from that of Paul. It is, indeed, rarely plausible to infer any considerable degree of direct Pauline influence in any of the Gospels, but in Matthew traces of such influence are indeed difficult to find ; and that Paul had read Matthew is plainly impossible. We may be tolerably sure that we have before us two writers independent of one another.

It is therefore of all the more interest to compare the treatment of certain Christian themes by these two writers, who in immediate background, angle of approach, and turn of mind appear to have so little in common. It is to such a comparison that I now turn.

I.   I propose to start with the eschatological framework of the Christian Gospel, which in its main lines is common to all parts of the New Testament. It has often been observed that the Epistles of Paul show a progressive diminution of interest in eschatology, while Matthew appears to have a place in a series which shows an ascending curve of interest. So far the two writers would seem to represent opposed tendencies. It has not, however, been so often observed that in one respect the two show a rather striking agreement. They both assign a special place in the eschatological scheme to the Kingdom of Christ, as in some sense distinct from the Kingdom of God.

Paul has left us a brief sketch of the eschatological sequence in I Cor. xv. There are three cardinal points : the Resurrection of Christ, His Advent, and τὸ τέλος. So he says, succinctly, in vv. 23–24. The τέλος, he adds, is the point at which Christ surrenders the βασιλεία to God the Father. He then explains that according to Scripture Christ must continue to reign (δεῖ βασιλεύειν) until He has put all His enemies beneath His feet, including the last enemy, Death. When this final conquest is complete, ' then the Son also will be subjected to Him who subjected all else to Him, that God may be all in all'. Such, we may take it, is the Kingdom of God in its final consummation. The Kingdom of Christ is in some sort a stage

towards that consummation. At which point His reign is
held to begin is not quite clear. It is certainly in being
between the παρουσία and the τέλος. It is not, however,
stated that it begins at the παρουσία. It may be legitimate
to adduce here a passage in Colossians—i. 12-14. Here
we are told that God the Father ' has made us capable
of a share in the inheritance of the saints in light '—the
inheritance being still future, but the act by which we are
made capable of it already past (for the verb is aorist).
In other words, He ' rescued us out of the dominion of
darkness and transferred us into the Kingdom of the Son
of His love, in whom we already enjoy the liberation which
is the forgiveness of sins '. This seems clear enough. The
divine act of redemption by which our sins are forgiven
has already admitted us to the Kingdom of Christ, while
it has also rendered us capable of entering hereafter into
the eternal light which is the Kingdom of God in its
fullness, which, as we are told in I Cor. xv. 50, flesh and
blood cannot inherit. It seems therefore that we are to
think of the Kingdom of Christ as inaugurated by His
Resurrection, to be manifested at His Advent, and finally
to pass into the consummated Kingdom of God.

The Gospel according to Matthew twice speaks of the
Kingdom of Christ in Marcan contexts where Mark does
not give the expression (xvi. 28, xx. 21). But the two
passages which are significant for our present purpose are
peculiar to Matthew : the interpretation of the Parable of
the Tares in xiii. 37-43, and the Judgment Scene of xxv.
31-46. In the former passage we read that at the συντέλεια
τοῦ αἰῶνος ' the Son of Man will send His angels, and they
will gather out of *His Kingdom* all scandals and those who
act lawlessly, and cast them ' (to resume the imagery of
the parable) ' into the furnace of fire. Then the righteous
will shine like the sun in *the Kingdom of their Father*.'. In
this climax we recognize once again the Kingdom of God
in its consummation—' the inheritance of the saints in
light ', according to Col. i. 12. Before the righteous enter
unto this final state, there has been a prior stage which is

called here, as by Paul, the Kingdom of Christ—more precisely, of the Son of Man. This Kingdom still contains righteous and unrighteous indistinguishably. It is the final Judgment which ends this provisional state, and leads to the consummation.

In xxv. 31–46 this Judgment is depicted in a dramatic scene. The Son of Man comes in glory attended by angels, and takes His throne. All nations are gathered before Him for judgment. As King, He pronounces sentence. The selfish and callous are dismissed to the eternal fire. To those who have served the King in the persons of His 'brethren' He says, ' Come, blessed of my Father, inherit the Kingdom prepared for you from the foundation of the world ' ; and thereupon they enter into eternal life. It is not here said that the kingdom they inherit (= eternal life) is the Kingdom of God, but we need hardly hesitate to make the identification. Those for whom the Kingdom has been prepared are the υἱοὶ τῆς βασιλείας of xiii. 38.

The parallel with Paul is close. For Matthew, as for Paul, the Kingdom of Christ exists in this world during historical time, under our familiar conditions with their confused mixture of evil and good. At what point, then, are we to suppose that Christ's reign begins ? It is at the Advent, according to xxv. 31, that He takes His throne, and the expressions, ' in his kingdom ', ' in thy kingdom ', in xvi. 28 and xx. 21, clearly refer to the same Advent. Yet in the closing verses of the Gospel the Risen Christ affirms that He is already invested with ἐξουσία ; by virtue of that authority He commissions His apostles to promulgate His commandments among all nations ; and at the same time He promises that He will be with them during the period still to elapse before the συντέλεια τοῦ αἰῶνος—which for Matthew is synchronous with the παρουσία. This Matthæan Christophany, in fact, as Professor R. H. Lightfoot has pointed out, is a kind of proleptic παρουσία, in sharp contrast to the Christophanies of Luke. The Resurrection is for Matthew the moment at which

Christ is invested with His Messianic kingship, and the promise of His continued presence with His followers indicates that they (His ' brethren ') form the community within which that kingship is effectively exercised. This is very close to the Pauline view. Both again agree that at Christ's advent His kingship will become effective over all mankind, in a final judgment to which, according to Matthew, ' all nations ' are exposed ; cf. Rom. ii. 12–16.

It is tempting to say, the Kingdom of Christ is the Church ; but the simple equation of the two is perhaps not justified. In Matthew the field in which wheat and tares grow together is the world where righteous and unrighteous are mingled until the King whose subjects they all are separates them ; and in the Judgment Scene we learn that over and above the ' brethren ' of the King —who are, in the first intention at least, members of the Church—there are many others who never knew Christ, and yet are, in the language of ch. xiii, υἱοὶ τῆς βασιλείας. Similarly, in Rom. ii. 12–16, on the day when God judges men through Christ, there will be Gentiles who knew not the Law, but did by nature the things of the Law, and who summon their consciences to witness before the throne. Are not they, we may ask, in some sense subjects of the Kingdom of Christ ? In neither case is it quite clear that we may absolutely identify the Kingdom of Christ with the Church, though the relation between the two concepts is very intimate.

II. This leads to a consideration of passages which deal directly with the Church. Matthew, alone of the Evangelists, uses the term ἐκκλησία. He uses it in the two senses which have been distinguished in Paul. In Matt. xviii. 17 ἡ ἐκκλησία means, *prima facie*, a local congregation ; in Matt. xvi. 18 ἡ ἐκκλησία μου is the Catholic Church, the new Israel. It may, however, be usefully recalled that there was at one time a local congregation which was also the whole congregation of Christian people in the world—the Church of Jerusalem. It appears (if

E

we may follow the Acts) that the use of the term ἡ ἐκκλησία, absolutely, for the Church of Jerusalem survived long after it had ceased to correspond with the facts (for example, Acts xviii. 22).   Christians elsewhere in Judæa, and later in Galilee and Samaria (Acts viii. 1, ix. 31), were regarded as non-resident members of ἡ ἐκκλησία, to wit, the Church of Jerusalem (while Paul spoke of αἱ ἐκκλησίαι τῆς Ἰουδαίας [Gal. i. 22]).   It may be, then, that we should read Matt. xviii. 17, which ostensibly refers to a local con-gregation, with the idea of the Catholic Church, or the new Israel, as an unexpressed extension of meaning.   I believe that the passage as a whole, xviii. 15–20, which is a kind of rudimentary ' Church Order ', demands such an extension.

It is, at any rate, here that we must start our comparison with Paul, for in view of the relations known to have existed between Peter and Paul, we shall hardly expect the epistles of the latter apostle to contain any echo of the statements of Matt. xvi. 18–19 that Peter holds the keys, and that he is the rock upon which the Church is founded. If Ephesians is Pauline, then Paul is prepared to speak of the apostolic body as a whole, together with the prophets, as the foundation of the Church (Eph. ii. 20) ; but else-where Christ is the Church's one foundation (I Cor. iii. 11) ; Peter and the others are pillars in the Temple, no more (Gal. ii. 9 ; cf. Rev. iii. 12).

If we turn, then, to xviii. 15–20 we find the ἐκκλησία depicted in the concrete as an organized society with its prescribed methods of discipline.   If one member offends, the offended person is to strive for reconciliation, first individually, and if that fails, with the support of one or two others.   In the last resort he must refer the matter to the ἐκκλησία.   If the offender is still contumacious, he is to be treated as excommunicate—ὥσπερ ὁ ἐθνικὸς καὶ ὁ τελώνης, a form of expression which certainly betrays a Jewish *milieu*.

Whatever be the original *Sitz im Leben* of these directions, we observe that Paul recommends substantially the same procedure. ' If a brother be overtaken by a fault, restore such an one in the spirit of meekness ' (Gal. vi. 1). This is no more than a paraphrase of Matt. xviii. 15. To act so, Paul adds, bearing one another's burdens, is to fulfil the ' law of Christ ' (Gal. vi. 2). If the effort is successful, according to Matthew, ἐκέρδησας τὸν ἀδελφόν. Κερδαίνειν in this sense is best illustrated by I Cor. ix. 19–22. It is found also in I Pet. iii. 1, and may be regarded as a quasi-technical term of early Christianity.

Where the attempt at reconciliation fails, recourse must be had, Paul enjoins, to the Church courts. In no case must a Christian cite a brother Christian before the secular courts (I Cor. v. 1–8). In the long-drawn-out case of the Corinthian offender (or offenders) we can see the procedure at work. The offender was to be excommunicated by vote of the ἐκκλησία (I Cor. v. 1–13). Apparently, however, this drastic step brought him to his senses, and in the upshot the offending brother was ' gained ' (II. Cor. ii. 5–11, vii. 10–13). The whole episode shows the Matthæan regulations, certainly Jewish Christian in form, at work in Paul's Gentile Christian churches.

To these disciplinary regulations Matthew has added a saying which empowers the apostles to ' bind and loose ', that is, to declare and enforce the laws of the Christian community. By implication, we must surely understand that the disciplinary action contemplated in the previous verses is to be carried out under apostolic authority. For Paul the question of apostolic authority is a delicate one, in view of his equivocal position *vis-à-vis* the Twelve. Dr. W. L. Knox (*St. Paul and the Church of Jerusalem*, 363 ff.) has shown that Paul's claim to be recognized as an apostle *in the same sense* as Peter and the rest of the Twelve was far from strong—no one, of course wished to deny him a place in the wider apostolic circle, with Barnabas, Andronicus and Junia, and others—and that he was un-comfortably aware of it. We may perhaps discern a cer-tain discomfort in his references to οἱ ὑπερλίαν ἀπόστολοι, οἱ δοκοῦντες, and the like (II Cor. xi. 5, xii. 11, Gal. ii.

1–10). Yet he had no wish to impugn apostolic authority in itself. His position was that he had received from Christ a commission as direct and as plenary as that of the Twelve, and that he possessed an authority equal to theirs to ' bind and loose ' in the name of Christ. ' I am writing ', he says, ' in my absence, in order that I may not have to come and deal summarily according to the authority which the Lord gave me ' (II Cor. xiii. 10). This authority he exercised, for example, in legislating for the conduct of Church assemblies in I Cor. xiv : ' If any one ', he adds (xiv. 37) ' claims to be a prophet or inspired person, let him recognize that what I write is of the Lord.[1] If he does not recognize it, he is not recognized.' Similarly in the Corinthian case of discipline, while the matter is adjudged by the ἐκκλησία, the sentence of excommunication is passed under Paul's apostolic authority : ' I have already decided ', he writes (ἤδη κέκρικα), ' as if I were present, you and my own spirit being assembled in the name of the Lord Jesus, to hand over the offender to Satan ' (I Cor. vv. 3–5).

᾿Εν τῷ ὀνόματι τοῦ Κυρίου ᾿Ιησοῦ συναχθέντων ὑμῶν : the expression recurs in the Matthæan passage, to which we now return. ' Where two or three are assembled in My name (συνηγμένοι εἰς τὸ ἐμὸν ὄνομα), there am I in their midst.' This may be understood to state the reason why, whether in the Jewish Christian community to which Matt. xviii. 15–20 is addressed, or in the Gentile Church of Corinth, the assembly of believers has the right to pass judgment on its own members : it is because Christ is among them since they are assembled in His name. But the saying in Matthew has also a larger reference. Its form cannot but recall the well-known maxim of *Pirqe Aboth* : ' When two sit and there are between them words of Torah, the Shekinah rests between them ' (*Pirqe Aboth*, iii. 3). It is difficult not to think that there is a connection between the two sayings. Although *Pirqe Aboth*, iii. 3 is

---

[1] ὅτι κυρίου ἐστιν : the ἐντολή, or ἐντολαί, of some MSS. is perhaps an interpolation.

attributed to R. Ḥanina ben Teradion, who was among the victims of the repression of Bar-Cochba's revolt, A.D. 135, and is therefore later than the First Gospel, yet any dependence of the Jewish saying upon the Christian is unlikely.[1] If we may assume that the idea expressed in Ḥanina's maxim underlies the Gospel saying, there is a twofold substitution : for the Torah as the link between two faithful Jews is substituted the name of Jesus as the principle of unity between two Christians ; and for the Shekinah—the divine Presence—is substituted Christ Himself in the midst of His people. This passage, therefore, which appears to set out to give nothing more than a kind of rudimentary Church-order, leads to a profound conception of what constitutes the ἐκκλησία : it is the body in which Christ dwells.

This interpretation is confirmed by the observation that a reiterated affirmation of Christ's presence in the Church forms the close and the climax of the whole Gospel (xxviii. 20). After the proclamation of the Kingdom of Christ (' All authority is given to Me ') the apostles are commissioned to promulgate the Law of Christ among all nations—i.e. the commission to ' bind and loose ' is given œcumenical scope—and the Gospel ends with the words, ' I am with you perpetually until the consummation of the age.' I should hazard the conjecture that the Evangelist may have written up this conclusion on the basis of the material he had given from an earlier source in ch. xviii. However that may be, the Church is clearly conceived as the *locus* of the presence of Christ on earth during the interval between His resurrection and παρουσία.

The full significance of this is to be appreciated only when we observe that the Gospel opens with the prophecy of ' Emmanuel, God with us,' just as it closes with the promise of Christ with us. In the view of this Evangelist,

[1] Ḥanina's maxim may be understood as meeting the peculiarly difficult situation during the Hadrianic persecution, when the Rabbinical schools were suppressed, and regular ordinations to the Rabbinate could not be carried on. Yet he was probably restating a principle anciently accepted.

the whole Gospel story is the story of how the presence of God came to men, first in the earthly ministry of Jesus, and then, through His resurrection, in the Church in which He dwells perpetually until the συντέλεια. The meaning of the saying in Matt. xviii. 20 becomes clearer when it is read in this context, although even by itself it implies clearly enough that the presence of Christ with His people is equivalent to the Shekinah.

Such is the high Matthæan doctrine of the Church. Its affinity with Paul's doctrine is manifest, even though the forms of expression are widely different. For Paul, the Church is the Body of Christ, in which He dwells by His Spirit. The Spirit of Christ, replacing the γράμμα of the Torah (II Cor. iii), provides the norm of life within the ἐκκλησία ; and as being also the Spirit of God, is the fulfilment of the prophetic promise which Matthew, though not Paul, expresses in the word Emmanuel. Within the Body of Christ, the individual member of the Church is in such sort identified with Christ that he can say Χριστῷ συνεσταύρωμαι, ζῶ δέ οὐκέτι ἐγὼ ζῇ δὲ ἐν ἐμοὶ Χριστός (Gal. ii. 19), and, again, ἀνταναπληρῶ τὰ ὑστερήματα τῶν θλίψεων τοῦ Χριστοῦ (Col. i. 24). Similarly in Matt. xxv. 40, 45 Christ says, ' Inasmuch as ye did it (did it not) to the least of these My brethren, ye did it (did it not) to Me.' We may recall that Dr. Albert Schweitzer found here the link between the historic teaching of Jesus and the Pauline ' Christ-mysticism '. At his conversion Paul heard the Lord saying, ' I am Jesus, whom you are persecuting ' (Act ix. 5, xxii. 8, xxvi. 15)—in other words, ' Inasmuch as you persecute My brethren, you do it to Me.' The idea of the solidarity of believers with the Lord is present in Paul's conversion experience, and the doctrine of the Body of Christ follows from it ; but that idea is already given in the sayings of Jesus as they appear in the Gospel according to Matthew.

III. In the Pauline Epistles and the First Gospel alike, the Christian position is stated in part by way of a polemical criticism of certain aspects of contemporary Judaism. Such criticism is to be found chiefly in the anti-Pharisaic discourse of Matt. xxiii and in the anti-Jewish *diatribé* of Rom. ii, though other passages in both authors may usefully be compared.

The Matthæan anti-Pharisaic discourse begins in a way which recalls curiously the opening of the Mishnic tractate *Pirqe Aboth*. The latter begins : ' Moses received the Torah from Sinai and delivered it to Joshua, and Joshua to the Elders, and the Elders to the Prophets, and the Prophets delivered it to the men of the Great Synagogue.' From them the succession of teachers is traced through various Rabbis to Hillel and Shammai, Gamaliel, and others, and so to Judah the Prince, the chief compiler of the Mishna. The intention is to assign to contemporary Rabbis the authority which is derived by a valid succession from Moses. Similarly the Matthæan discourse begins : ' The scribes and the Pharisees sit in Moses' seat ; all therefore that they command you, do and keep.' This introduction conclusively points to a Jewish *milieu* (whether it be the Judaism of the time of Jesus or a Jewish-Christian community). It is only after this entirely orthodox introduction that, by a kind of *paraprosdokia*, the discourse turns to denunciation of these successors of Moses.

To speak broadly, six main charges are brought against them, which we may enumerate as follows :

(1) Their conduct is inconsistent with their teaching.
(2) They lay burdens on others which they do not bear themselves.
(3) They glorify themselves as teachers.
(4) They refuse to enter the Kingdom of God and prevent others from entering.
(5) They care for the outward and neglect the inward.
(6) They repeat the murder of the prophets, while professing to honour them.

The Pauline passage is different in form and manner. Its style is that of the Hellenistic *diatribé*, with its pointed

apostrophes and its free use of the rhetorical question.   In
substance, however, the charges which Paul brings against
the Jews in general are similar to those to which the
scribes and Pharisees are exposed in Matthew.

The charges numbered 1, 2, 3, and 5 are represented
by fairly close parallels in Romans.

(1) Paul charges the Jews whom he has in mind with
claiming to know the will of God, to possess the formula
of knowledge and truth in the Torah, and to teach its
precepts, while acting contrary to them (Rom. ii. 17–23).
Not the hearers of the Law, he reminds them, but the
doers are justified before God (Rom. ii. 13 ; cf. Matt. vii.
15–21).

(2) They pronounce judgment on others, while evading
it themselves.   The wording of Rom. ii. 1–3 echoes
Matt. vii. 1 seq., while the development of the charge at
length in vv. 21–23 is similar in substance to Matthew's
charge of laying on others φορτία which they refuse to
touch themselves (xxiii. 4).   In Gal. vi. 2–5, on the contrary, the Law of Christ (by implication) demands that
every man shall bear his own φορτίον.

(3) As in Matt. xxiii 5–10 the scribes pride themselves
on the title Rabbi (or in Greek καθηγητής), so the Jew
who is the butt of Paul's attack (Rom. ii. 19–20) professes
to be ὁδηγὸς τυφλῶν (cf. Matt. xv. 14, xxiii. 16), φῶς τῶν ἐν
σκότει (cf. Matt. v. 14–16), παιδευτὴς ἀφρόνων, διδάσκαλος
νηπίων.

(5) The charge of caring for externals at the expense
of the inward life (Matt. xxiii. 25–28) has its parallel in
Rom. ii. 28–29, where ὁ ἐν τῷ φανερῷ Ἰουδαῖος is contrasted with ὁ ἐν τῷ κρυπτῷ Ἰουδαῖος.   For the terms used,
cf. Matt. vi. 16–18, where the cognate verb φανῆναι and
adjective κρυφαῖος convey the same meanings.

For the other two charges, those of preventing men
from entering the Kingdom of God and of being accessory
to the murder of the prophets, we must turn to I Thess. ii.
15–16, where the Jews are charged with killing the Lord
Jesus and the prophets and with preventing the preaching

of salvation to the Gentiles. As in Matthew the accumulated guilt of the murder of the righteous in all ages rests upon this generation (xxiii. 34–36), so Paul declares that the Jews have now completed the tale of their sins (ἀναπληρῶσαι αὐτῶν τὰς ἁμαρτίας), and the wrath has come upon them finally (εἰς τέλος). Without any verbal resemblance, the inner affinity of the two passages is close.

It appears that behind Paul's polemic there lies a tradition of anti-Judaic, or anti-Pharisaic, propaganda very similar in general purport to that which we find in Matthew. What is particularly remarkable is that both Matt. xxiii and Rom. ii. have the character of criticism of Judaism from a standpoint within Judaism, rather than an attack from without. None of the charges, whether in Matthew or in Paul, presupposes distinctively Christian principles or standards : all of them might have been brought against Jews by a Jew who believed that his nation and his faith were being put to shame by unworthy representatives of them.

IV. To sum up : comparison of certain passages in the First Gospel and in the Pauline Epistles reveals significant agreements between them in eschatological teaching, in the idea of the Church and Church-order, and in the controversy with Pharisaic Judaism. There is nothing to suggest either literary dependence or derivation from a common written source ; but it would appear that behind both writers there lies some kind of common tradition. It is a tradition notably Jewish-Christian in character, whether we meet it in Matthew or in Paul. We are apt to forget that the apostle to the Gentiles was himself a Jewish Christian. He was, in fact, precisely what Matthew describes in xiii. 52, a Rabbi converted [1] to the Christian religion. Of his early career as a Christian we know

---

[1] Μαθητευθείς is in the Peshitta mettalmad : talmēd is in Syriac writers the technical term for to ' convert ' a person to a faith, a philosophy, or a way of life. Μαθητεύειν is similarly used in Matt. xxviii. 19 : we may fairly conjecture that it represents the expression used in the early Aramaic-speaking Church.

singularly little. For several years after his conversion, he tells us, he was unknown by face to the churches of Judæa (Gal. i. 22). That is not to say that he was out of touch with the synagogue or with Christians of Jewish origin. Among his friends, Andronicus and Junia at least were Jews converted to Christianity before Paul himself (Rom. xvi. 7). Moreover, in his sketch of an autobiography in II Cor. xi. 24 he tells us that he was five times beaten by the Jews. He must at that time have been subject to synagogal discipline. It is probable that a great part of his twelve years' ministry (or so) in the κλίματα of Syria and Cilicia (Gal. i. 21) was exercised within the framework of the synagogue. There is no need for the doubts which have been expressed about the statement of Acts that even after the opening of his Gentile mission from Antioch he still started whenever possible in the synagogue. The *diatribé* of Rom. ii. might well be a product of his early years when the Jewish colouring of the environment in which he worked was still pronounced.

It appears, therefore, that we are being led back to a very early stage in the formation of the Christian tradition, before any marked divergence between the ideas of Jewish and Gentile Christianity had developed. The material we have examined has the character of διδαχή as distinct from κήρυγμα. Both traditional forms, the ' didactic ' and the ' kerygmatic ', certainly go back to the earliest times. It may be that we have been tracing one more way of approach to that central and primitive tradition in which we must seek a firm base for the exploration of the life and teaching of Jesus.

4. THE MIND OF PAUL : I

(1933)

'A STURDY little bald-headed, bow-legged man, with meeting eyebrows and a rather prominent nose.'[1] Such is the description of the Apostle Paul which has been handed down by tradition. And it is quite likely a good tradition, for although the document in which it occurs has late elements, yet there are good reasons for putting the tradition itself back to the early second century, or even to the first ; and it belongs to a region where the memory of Paul was especially cherished—his own ' Galatia '.[2] In any case, there are allusions in the epistles which confirm the main lines of the picture. It is evident that Paul was of insignificant appearance, for his enemies at Corinth twitted him with it, and there was enough truth in the charge to give it a sting.[3] Paul was conscious that he did not look impressive ; and he resented it. That is not only a physical but also a psychological *datum*. But the tradition also avers that he was εὐεκτικός, well knit, or in good condition—a sturdy little man. It is often supposed that Paul was a sickly person. It is true that he several times alludes to illness. But we have only to consider the list of adventures and sufferings in II. Cor. xi. 23–32, to realize that this was no semi-invalid or valetudinarian. Five times scourged within an inch of his life (for thirty-nine stripes is the savage maximum penalty), once stoned, with nearly fatal results,[4] shipwrecked on four occasions,[5] on one of which he suffered twenty-four hours' exposure in the open sea—he must have been pretty tough. Of his

[1] Acts of Paul and Thecla, § 3.
[2] See the discussion of these *Acta* in W. M. Ramsay, *The Church in the Roman Empire*, pp. 31 *sqq.*
[3] II Cor. x. 10–11.
[4] II Cor. xi. 25 may safely be identified with Acts xiv. 19.
[5] To the three shipwrecks mentioned in II Cor. xi. 25 we must add the (later) shipwreck of Acts xxvii 39–44.

recurrent malady—if such it was—we know little. He
was ill at the time when he first preached in Galatia.[1]
He felt himself to be a pitiable object, and was grateful to
the Galatians for not treating him with contempt.[2] In
II Cor. xii. 7 he speaks of being ' battered ' by an illness
as painful as a ' stake in the flesh ', and this illness was
either persistent or recurrent, for he adds ' I prayed to the
Lord about it three times, that it might leave me,' but
apparently his prayer was not answered. Just before
writing II Cor. i. 8–9, his life had been despaired of ; and
this seems more likely to have been due to severe illness
(probably an attack of the same malady) than to persecution. That is all we really know. Diagnosis is impossible.[3] But we may fairly say that he was a man of generally sound constitution and great resistant and recupera-
tive powers, but suffering from some physical disability
which from time to time checked his efficiency and hindered
his work. This disability he resented bitterly. It was ' a
messenger of Satan '.[4] He felt it an intolerable humiliation, thwarting his purposes, and exposing him to contempt.

So much we know of the man's physical constitution.
What of that half-physical, half-psychical thing, temperament ? It is clear that he was what is called highly-strung
—sensitive to conditions, a man of moods, with emotions
readily aroused. The emotional temperament is reflected
in his literary style. At its best it is elevated, moving, and
impassioned ; at its worst, involved or incoherent. It is
seldom or never level, cool, or tame. His letters betray
his varying moods. In I Thess. ii. 17–iii. 5, for example,
he appears agitated and worried, resentful of hindrances,

---

[1] Gal. iv. 13. Δι'ἀσθένειαν τῆς σαρκός can scarcely bear any other meaning
than ' because of bodily illness '.

[2] Gal. iv. 14. To attempt to identify a disease which makes the sufferer
loathsome is to misunderstand the passage completely. The sense of humiliation is wholly in Paul's own mind. The Galatians, being ordinarily decent
people, felt pity, not contempt.

[3] There is no evidence for the diagnosis of epilepsy, which once had
a vogue : nor can we fairly use Gal. iv. 15, still less Gal. vi. 11, as evidence
for ophthalmia.

[4] II Cor. xii. 7.

impatient with waiting.   In those days, as he tells us in
retrospect in I Cor. ii. 1–5, he was in a state of abject
nervousness, which made him incapable of effective speech
just when he would have wished to be most effective.   Yet
at other times he had the orator's sense of power and
delight in swaying an audience—' demolishing arguments,
and all arrogance that affronts the knowledge of God,
and leading captive every thought into the allegiance of
Christ '.[1]   That he had a hot and quick temper Galatians
and II Corinthians sufficiently prove, and the converse,
his capacity for warm affection and craving for its return,
is evident in most of the letters.   Sometimes he wears his
heart upon his sleeve.[2]   Having this ardent temperament,
he took life seriously, with little of that saving sense of
humour which for many men lightens the burden of things.
Now and again in his letters, perhaps, he will be playful,
but it is a rather heavy playfulness at best.   This was
temperamental, and certainly not due to any slowness of
wit, for his intelligence was nimble enough.   His mind
leaps with almost embarrassing quickness from one aspect
of an idea to another, and his rapid parentheses and asides
are among the most marked features of his style.   Corresponding to his sensitiveness to emotional stimulus was an
openness to intellectual impressions which gives a rich
variety to his presentation of Christian thought.   Without
it he would not have been so effective an interpreter of
Christianity to the thinking world of his time—or so teasing
to his modern interpreters.

To this we must add that he had that kind of spiritual
constitution (whatever it may be) that makes the mystic.
The question whether or not Paul's theology is rightly
described as mystical is perhaps largely a matter of definition.   But his allusion to a rapture to Paradise [3] indicates
a type of experience which is characteristic of mysticism.

[1] II Cor. x. 4–6.
[2] E.g. I Thess. ii. 7–8, II Cor. vi. 11–vii. 7 (omitting vi. 14–vii. 1, which
is probably a misplaced page of another letter).   The absence of conven-
tional reserve in such passages is characteristic.
[3] II Cor. xii. 4.

There is no reason to suppose that such experiences began for him with his Christian life. On the contrary, it is probable that his Christianity tended to control and moderate the mystical impulse and to re-direct it into more profitable channels. All his life the unseen world must have been to him an immediate and impressive reality,[1] and he was easily ready, as most of us are not, to find motives and satisfactions in the spiritual world.

So much we seem justified in setting down as defining Paul's native constitution. What can we further know of the conditions which influenced his early life? We are told by his biographer that he was of Tarsus, and the statement need hardly be questioned. With this clue we can recognize at once the influence of city life upon his early mind. It has often been observed that while Jesus was a man of the country, Paul was a man of the town. He scarcely betrays any feeling for the beauty or pathos of the natural world. He does, indeed, speak of the creation groaning and travailing in pain ; but it has never occurred to him to dwell upon the fall of the sparrow or the withering of the grass. 'Does God care for cattle?' he asks with a scornful incredulity.[2] His one attempt to draw a detailed illustration from agricultural life—the allegory of the grafted olive [3]—only proves his ignorance of it. On the other hand his mind is full of images of city life. The market, the law-court, the race-course, the army supply his illustrations ; and if many of his metaphors in this department are part of the rhetorical commonplace of the time, that very fact links him with the environment in which he, like the popular preachers of Stoicism and Cynicism, was at home—the environment of the Greek city-state.

We are further informed by that companion of Paul whose journal is used in the second part of the Acts of the Apostles, that he was a Roman citizen. The statement again is entirely credible, although it is not directly confirmed by his letters. It gives us, however, a clue to the

---

[1] II Cor. iv. 18.   [2] I Cor. ix. 9.   [3] Rom. xi. 17–24.

œcumenical outlook which distinguished him from many early Christian teachers. If he was a Roman citizen, as well as a citizen of Tarsus, then we may conclude that his family was of some social standing—and that in a world where social standing counted for at least as much as it did in this country before the death of Queen Victoria. For in the first century the imperial policy confined the coveted privilege of citizenship in the provinces to the landed gentry and the municipal aristocracy. It is true that he is recorded in the Acts to have been a tent-maker by trade, and some have thought that this places him in what we call the working class. But it was a point of honour among good Jews that a man who occupied himself with the Torah should have a trade by which he could live, that he might not be tempted to make his calling in the Law a source of profit. That he was not born to a ' proletarian ' status seems clear from the tone of his letters. A man born to manual labour does not speak self-consciously of ' labouring with my own hands '. Consider the sarcastic outburst of I Cor. iv. 9–13 :

I think God has exhibited us apostles as the lowest of the low, like gallows-birds ; for we have become a spectacle to the universe, both angels and men. We are fools for Christ's sake, while you are most prudent Christians ; we are feeble while you are strong ; we are in disgrace while you are honoured. To this very moment we are starving, thirsty, ragged, battered tramps. We toil at labour with our own hands. Vilified, we give good words ; hunted down, we endure ; slandered, we make our meek appeal. We are like the dregs and scum of society to this very moment !

Surely we miss the point of this unless we read it as the utterance of one whose natural place in society is the exact reverse of all this. Most illuminating of all, perhaps, is Phil. iv. 15–19. Here Paul is trying to say a graceful word of thanks for a gift of money. How much he hated taking it, we may infer from I Cor. ix. 15–18. He can scarcely bring himself to acknowledge that the money was welcome to him, and covers up his embarrassment by piling up technical terms of trade,[1] as if to give the transaction a severely 'business' aspect. This was a man who had chosen poverty as his lot for ideal ends, but could never feel himself one of the ' poor ', to whom alms might be offered without suspicion of offence. He was indeed no aristocrat, but he had the feelings of a well-to-do *bourgeois*.[2]

Paul, therefore—and this is of importance for his development—started with a secure position in the cosmopolitan society of his time. But there was one flaw in his title : he was a Jew, of pure Hebrew descent and strict Jewish upbringing. We are to understand, probably, that his parents spoke Aramaic and taught it to their children : [3] not all Jews of the Dispersion did that. These were Jews with a strongly national outlook. They brought up their son as a Pharisee. Thus, Roman citizen as he was, he was nevertheless uncompromisingly a Jew. Now a Jew might be wealthy, he might have an influential social position, but he belonged to a minority, an intensely self-conscious minority, and an unpopular minority. The Jew of the Dispersion was so constantly kept in mind of the contempt with which others regarded him, that he had to be continually reminding himself that he belonged to the chosen people of God, possessed of a dignity before which the pomp of emperors paled. The self-consciousness of the Jew was deeply engrained in Paul's mind : it must have entered with his earliest impressions. In his letters, written in middle age, he comes before us as the champion of a supra-national religion. His watchword is ' There is no distinction.' Yet to the end of his life it remained to him a miracle, a ' mystery ', that Jew and Gentile could meet on common ground.[4] The miracle had happened, but it remained a miracle. We may infer

---

[1] εἰς λόγον δόσεως καὶ λήψεως, τὸν καρπόν τὸν πλεονάζοντα, εἰς λόγον ὑμῶν, ἀπέχω, πεπλήρωμαι.

[2] Here I follow W. M. Ramsay against Adolf Deissmann.

[3] Ἑβραῖος ἐξ Ἑβραίων Phil. iii. 5, cf. Acts vi. 1, where Ἑβραῖος is clearly the contrary of Ἑλληνιστής, Greek speaking.

[4] Eph. i. 15–ii. 22, Col. i. 21–29, foreshadowed already in Rom. xv. 7–13.

from this the intensity of his national feeling in his earliest
days. There was material for a very acute conflict between Saul the Jew, and Paul, the Roman of Tarsus.

We picture him then growing up at Tarsus. His keen
intellectual curiosity, his interest in the human scene, his
sensitiveness to impressions, drew him outwards towards
the busy life of Græco-Roman society. Was he not a
Roman, and did he not belong to it? Not less, his sym-
pathetic temperament, his warm-hearted capacity for
affection, must have lured him into the fellowship of his
Gentile contemporaries. Our evidence for his Gentile
friendships belongs, of course, to his later life as a Christian,
but he surely had it in him from the first to enter into these
wider relationships. Yet there was a great gulf fixed.
Even if he had been willing to forget it, society would not
allow him to do so. But he could not forget it, and did
not wish to forget it. He 'gloried' in it. That word
(καυχᾶσθαι with its derivates καύχημα, καύχησις) has an
important place in Paul's vocabulary.[1] It was a necessity
for him to have something to be proud of. That is not
necessarily anything unworthy. Without being able to
identify himself with something of which he can be proud
—his country, his profession, or what not—a man is a poor
creature. Yet a less admirable kind of pride easily creeps
in, the more so if there is any factor in the man's experience
that suggests humiliation. And Paul, as we have seen,
was sensitive to humiliation. He must have a καύχημα, a
ground of pride. And what should that be but the glory
of Israel?

If anyone thinks he has ground for self-confidence in his
natural advantages, I can beat him there—circumcised the
eighth day, Israelite by descent, of the tribe of Benjamin,
Hebrew-speaking and of a Hebrew-speaking family ; in regard
to the Torah, a Pharisee.[2]

Paul had been a Christian for some thirty years when he

---

[1] καυχᾶσθαι, καύχησις, καύχημα occur over 50 times, and in every epistle
except II Thessalonians, Colossians and Philemon.

[2] Phil. iii. 4–5.

F

wrote that. How strong must that pride have been forty
years earlier? The social and religious integrity of Israel
—all that the Torah stood for—came to be the ideal about
which all his faculties and interests were organized in a
dominant sentiment of great power and tenacity. The
more his curiosity and sympathy led him to know the pagan
environment, the more sharply was his contrasted ideal
defined, and the more intensely were his emotions evoked
for the service of that ideal.

That meant further that his whole inward comfort and
satisfaction must depend on living up to the demands of
his ideal. The Torah was a comprehensive religious and
ethical system : it was a norm of belief, a liturgy of worship, a mould for spiritual experience and aspiration, but
above all it was a code of rules for conduct (*Halacha*).
For Paul certainly it was that above all. His regular
equivalent for the Hebrew ' *torah* ' is the narrower Greek
term νόμος, ' law ' ; and he emphasizes this aspect of the
Torah by frequently using the even more precise term
ἐντολή, ' commandment '. We cannot doubt that this
represents the aspect in which religion had been impressed
upon him from childhood. It was first and foremost an
ethical imperative, expressed in detailed rules of behaviour.
His upbringing must have been strict and austere. We
shall not go far wrong in reading through the formalized
outline of Rom. vii. 7 *sqq.* a vivid personal recollection.[1]
' Once upon a time (and how long ago it seems !) I lived
my own life, and Law was not there.' Is there any more
apt description of a very little child—following its instinctive impulses without thought of restraint ? ' But when
the Commandment came, Sin sprang to life—and I was
dead ! ' The instincts are beginning to be repressed. As
the boy matures, the repression is not merely administered
from without : it is inwardly accepted. ' I delight in the
Law in my inner self.' His pride and honour are engaged
in the keeping of the Law—the glory of Israel. If he was

---

[1] See introductory note to this passage in my Commentary on
Romans.

to have any καύχημα—any pride, confidence or satisfaction
in life—it must be through the Law.

Jewish critics find something rather morbid or abnormal
about Paul's attitude to the Law.   Other Pharisees did
not feel as he did.   But there is a phrase in his letter to
the Galatians (i. 14) which betrays the reason for this
departure from the normal : ' I was forging ahead in
Judaism beyond many of my contemporaries, for I was
extraordinarily keen about my ancestral traditions.'   There
we have the personal factor added to the impersonal pride
in the glory of Israel—Paul must at all costs excel.   He
creates for himself an ideal of scrupulous perfection which
to many of his fellow-Pharisees must have seemed fantastic.   No wonder his moral conflict was so desperate.
Naturally hot passions were being ruthlessly repressed by
a fanatical ideal, an ideal which summoned to its support
not only the highest spiritual affections of a mystic, but the
instinctive impulses associated with personal, family and
racial pride and honour.   We need not be surprised either
that the conflict often went against his dominant sentiment, or that when so betrayed he felt in despair, ' It is
not I that do the deed, but Sin that dwells in me '—a
demonic power rising out of unconscious depths like a
devil from the Pit.   It is an evidence of the man's complete sincerity, and of his power of self-analysis, that the
command he cites as bringing him to despair is Οὐκ
ἐπιθυμήσεις—' Thou shalt not covet ' (or ' lust '—the
Greek word covers both).   His acts, he found, he might
control, but not his desires ; and the more he tried to
repress them, the more insistent they became.   ' I should
never have known what it was to covet and lust, but that
the Law said : Thou shalt not covet ; but Sin found its
opportunity in that command, and evoked all kinds of lust
and covetousness in me.'

Here are the conditions of the inner conflict portrayed
in Rom. vii.   We are accustomed to treat it as an example
of the universal experience of moral struggle, and we have
a right to do so.   But in Paul's case the struggle was

determined by peculiar conditions. The Law was not simply 'the moral law' in a general sense. It was the symbol of the glory of Israel which gave him self-respect before the world. Among the forces opposed to it were not only temptations to moral transgressions which the general sense of mankind would recognize as such, but also temptations to a freer association with the great world of which he would gladly have been a part, and inclinations to equal and friendly intercourse with Gentiles. Paul the Roman and Saul the Jew were at strife.

> They cease not fighting, east and west
>   On the marches of my breast.
> Here the truceless armies yet
>   Trample, rolled in blood and sweat ;
> They kill and kill and never die ;
>   And I think that each is I.

Now when a severe conflict exists within the self, one way of relief is to externalize the conflict by identifying that which one detests in oneself with some other person or body of persons. How much of the persecuting intolerance in the world, even to-day, might be traced to such an origin ? Paul found relief in persecuting the Nazarenes. In doing so, he was gratifying his desire to excel in the service of the Law. In both of the passages in his letters where he recites his distinctions as a Jew (Gal. i. 14, Phil. iii. 4–6), he makes his persecution of the Church the supreme test of his 'zeal'. We may be sure that the principal reason why he could embrace this grim task was that here were enemies of the Law whom he could smite as he was failing to smite the enemies of the Law in his own breast. The 'blasphemies' of the Nazarenes made it easy to find in them an embodiment of that 'other law, warring against the Law of my mind'. By speaking lightly of the Torah and the Temple, and hailing the Messiah in a dead criminal, they were dragging the glory of Israel in the mire. The repressed passions of his nature found a consecrated outlet here : the 'threatenings and slaughter' which he breathed out promised to cleanse his

bosom of much perilous stuff. In many of the Psalms of
the canonical Psalter, and of ' Solomon ', we may find his
attitude depicted : ' Lord, how I love Thy Law,' is
balanced by ' Do I not hate them, O Lord, which hate
Thee ? I hate them with a perfect hatred ! '

We may here pause to consider the spiritual conditions
represented by these facts. It is often thought that Paul is
making fantastic or exaggerated statements when he speaks
of the Law as the means of sin and death. But his state
of mind was in fact extremely pernicious. He had wholly
identified himself (in intention) with a certain ideal, represented by the Torah interpreted as a peculiarly meticulous
code of precepts. So fully had he identified himself with
it that unless he could see himself as the perfect Pharisee,
life lost meaning. He had staked all on his καύχημα, his
pride in the Law. At the same time he was aware that
this picture of himself as the perfect Pharisee was denied
by facts of his own experience. It was fantasy, not reality.
Every effort he could make within the bounds of the Torah
was only deepening the cleft which divided his soul in two.
The expedient of consecrating himself to a holy war against
the Nazarenes could not finally deliver him from this
division in the self. We cannot imagine such a man as
Paul finding permanent satisfaction in hatred—if indeed
any man could ever find it. His humane impulses must
have put up a good fight. Perhaps one reason why his
career came to a stop before the gates of Damascus was
sheer revulsion from his task—a task nevertheless set him,
as he believed, by the God who gave the Law.

Any inquiry into the methods and stages of Paul's conversion must be mainly speculative. He was unconscious
of them himself, for to him the whole thing was the sudden
blinding flash that decided the issue. What we have to
do is to try to define the meaning of his conversion as the
solution of the conflict which was ruining his life. It
meant the abandonment of that fantasy of himself as the
perfect Pharisee by which he had hitherto been controlled.
It meant that he accepted the plain fact that he did not,

and could not, keep the Law of God. Thus his *καύχημα*, his pride and self-respect, was gone. ' My advantages I counted disadvantages.' [1] He was thrown upon the great world to stand or fall without any of the moral and spiritual support which a Jew gained from his Torah. He threw in his lot with One irretrievably cursed by the Law : ' Cursed be everyone that is hanged on a tree. . . . I have been crucified with Christ.' [2] That meant something tragically final for a Pharisee. There was no getting past it : he was outside the Law, no better than ' sinners of the Gentiles '.[3] That did not mean that he renounced the high ethical ideal represented by the Law as interpreted by the Pharisees. He was now, said he, not *ἄνομος Θεοῦ*, but *ἔννομος Χριστοῦ* (' not God's outlaw, but Christ's in-law ',[4] if we are to keep the play upon words). Having seen ' the light of the knowledge of God's glory in the face of Jesus Christ ',[5] he had entered into a more inclusive, more absolute conception of the will of God than the Law could give. This is not the place to attempt any more precise theological definition of the consequences of this. What we have to observe is that pride in the Law has been displaced by pride in the Cross ; pride in ' righteousness ' as an achievement, by pride in that which empties him of pride. ' God forbid that I should glory save in the Cross of our Lord Jesus Christ by which the world has been crucified to me, and I to the world.' [6] ' Where is pride ? It is excluded.' [7] We shall not wonder at this emphasis on the exclusion of pride if we realize that it was just here that Paul's conflict came to its issue. In glorifying the Law he had thought to glorify himself—' in regard to legal righteousness, blameless ' [8]—and the shame of breaking it was breaking him down. Now the conflict was resolved. He accepted his failure, and trusted God to work in him

---

[1] Phil. iii. 7.   [2] Gal. iii. 13, ii. 19.   [3] Gal. ii. 15.
[4] I Cor. ix. 21.   [5] II Cor. iv. 6.
[6] Gal. vi. 14.   [7] Rom. iii. 27.
[8] Phil. iii. 6. This need not be understood as a contradiction of the confession in Rom. vii. The point of view is different. The valuation of *κέρδη* in Phil. iii. is *ἐν σαρκί*.

that which was well-pleasing to Himself. The result was a sense of freedom and expansion, which is manifest in all his writings, and is a sure sign of a soul at unity with itself and reconciled to God and man. All his powers and capacities were released and his wide sympathies given free play ; for with the Law had gone that ' middle wall of partition ' [1] which had separated him from his fellow-men. He might love and serve them, Jew and Greek alike, without restraint or misgiving. Thus the universality of his mission was given, at least implicitly, in the fact of his conversion.

In essentials, the new way of life was determined for Paul by the crisis that brought him into Christianity. It would be easy to illustrate in detail its effects in particular moral situations. His liberation, however, was not at once complete. In his earlier letters (the earliest of which are not less than fifteen years later than his conversion) we find indications that old ways of thought and traits of character in part survived the change, and were only gradually brought captive to the allegiance of Christ. There is a touchiness about his dignity which sorts ill with the selflessness of one who has died with Christ. When opposition presents itself, he will override it ' with a rod '.[2] When external conditions thwart him, he resents it.[3] When illness or nervous exhaustion reduces his efficiency, he chafes and frets.[4] Unconsciously, perhaps, he still yields to the desire to excel : he must feel himself better, stronger, more efficient, wiser in spiritual things, than others. He must observe counsels of perfection he would not recommend to all.[5] There is a revealing touch in I Cor. ix. 15. Paul is replying to criticisms that have been passed upon his attitude in the matter of receiving relief from the Church. He affirms that by Scripture and by the word of Christ he has every right to be paid ; that he is every bit as good

---

[1] Eph. ii. 14.
[2] I Cor. iv. 21.   [3] ' Satan hindered us ', I Thess. ii. 18.
[4] ' A messenger of Satan to batter me ', II Cor. xii. 7.
[5] I Cor. vii. 8–9.

as Peter and others who did take pay ; but that he forbears to use his right—and why ? ' No one shall stultify my pride (καύχημα) ; I'd rather die ! '

All this means that Paul had not yet fully carried through the process which he knew well was the only logical issue of his conversion. He had not made that final abandonment of any claim upon life for personal and individual pride and satisfaction which is involved in the surrender to God in Christ. Hence there are still elements in life, in the ways of Providence, in his own experience, to which he is not fully reconciled. Apparently it needed a further spiritual crisis to bring him right through. This crisis seems to be reflected in II Corinthians, and most clearly reflected if we accept the very widely held critical view that this epistle is composed out of parts of two letters (with perhaps a fragment of a third in vi. 14–vii. 1). On this view, chs. x–xiii were written earlier than the first nine chapters.

The situation then works out thus. Paul had had trouble with the Corinthian Church. He resolved to pay a flying visit from Ephesus, confident that he had only to appear in person in order to re-establish his authority. He was disappointed. His opponents carried the majority of the Church with them, and he found himself incapable of effective speech or action. He returned to Ephesus smarting under bitter humiliation.[1] In a passion of resentment he wrote a letter full of caustic sarcasm and indignant self-vindication. This letter is represented by II Cor. x–xiii. In Ch. xi he lets himself go—and comments ' I speak as a fool.' At least he had the grace to realize it ! And moreover the same letter shows how in the depth of his humiliation he found firm ground. ' I am strong just when I am weak.'[2] That is not mere ' paradox '. It has profound psychological truth. So long as he

---

[1] ταπεινός, ταπεινοῦν, II Cor. x. 1, xi. 7, xii. 21, are the words he used ; and ταπεινός in the mouth of a Greek was an insult ; it was a *tour de force* of Christianity to make ' humility ' a virtue.

[2] II Cor. xii. 10.

chafed against unavoidable disabilities and reverses which wounded his prestige, he was losing the spiritual liberty and power which come from the abandonment of personal claims. But when he accepted his limitations he was liberated afresh. It is likely that he was ill at the time he wrote, and that before he recovered he came near death.[1] When he wrote again (II Cor. i–ix), it was in a strangely chastened mood. It is not only that he apologizes for the tone of his previous letter, and pleads for a restoration of his Corinthian friends' alienated affection. He also makes it plain that he has gone to the depths and made terms with the last realities. There is nothing in earlier letters like the quiet self-abandonment of II Cor. iv–v.

Whether or not I am right in isolating this particular spiritual crisis as a sort of second conversion, it is at any rate plain that in the later epistles [2] there is a change of temper. The traces of fanaticism and intolerance disappear, almost if not quite completely, along with all that anxious insistence on his own dignity. The new temper shows itself in the way in which the controversies of Romans and Colossians are conducted, in a generous recognition of the natural virtues of mankind,[3] in a sense of the values of ordinary family life [4] (which he had once deprecated as belonging to ' the things of the world ') [5] and in a sustained emphasis on the idea of reconciliation. It is in the epistle to the Philippians (possibly the last of his letters which we possess in an uninterpolated form) that we see most clearly what experience had made of this naturally proud, self-assertive, and impatient man. 'I do not reckon myself', he says, ' to have attained. . . . I am pressing on towards the mark.' [6] And he adds, ' Let

[1] Cf. II Cor. i. 8.

[2] I assume, with most critics, that the letters fall chronologically as follows : (i) the Thessalonian correspondence, (ii) the Corinthian correspondence, (iii) Romans, (iv) the Captivity Epistles. Galatians I should place along with the Corinthian epistles in group (ii) ; some would date it earlier. Recently proposals have been made for dating the Captivity Epistles earlier. These are discussed in the next paper.

[3] Rom. ii. 14–15, xiii. 1–7.   [4] Col. iii. 18–21, Eph. v. 22–vi. 4.
[5] I Cor. vii. especially 32–4.   [6] Phil. iii. 13–14.

those of us who are mature take this view. If anyone takes a different view on any matter, God will make that matter plain to him. Only we must go by the principle at which we have arrived.' [1] And when he thinks of the hardships he has endured, and the final sufferings which now impend, he no longer complains of the ' messenger of Satan to batter me ' ; he no longer ' glories ' in his exceptional afflictions, as he once did (speaking ' as a fool ') ; he is content to take things as they come. ' I have learned to find satisfaction in the circumstances in which I am placed : I know how to be humiliated ; [2] I also know how to enjoy plenty. I have been initiated into life as a whole and into all its several experiences.' [3] His mind dwells upon ' all that is true, all that is reverend, all that is just, all that is pure, all that is lovely, all that is of good repute—all virtue and all praise ',[4] and ' the peace of God which passes all understanding ' is the ' garrison ' of his heart.[5]

---

[1] Phil. iii. 15–16.   It is regrettable that the A.V. here follows an inferior text, which transforms this expression of a wide tolerance into a plea for uniformity.

[2] $\tau\alpha\pi\epsilon\iota\nu\circ\tilde{\upsilon}\sigma\theta\alpha\iota$.   In II Cor. xi. 7, xii. 21, the word is used with bitterness of Paul's humiliation at Corinth, and the adjective $\tau\alpha\pi\epsilon\iota\nu\acute{\circ}\varsigma$ similarly in II Cor. x. 1.   To be $\tau\alpha\pi\epsilon\iota\nu\acute{\circ}\varsigma$ is for Paul, as for the Greeks, something naturally distasteful.   But he has learned to accept it.

[3] Phil. iv. 11–12.   [4] Phil. iv. 8–9.   [5] Phil. iv. 7.

5. THE MIND OF PAUL: II

(1934)

THERE has been much discussion in recent years of the question whether or not it is possible to trace any development in the thought of Paul as it is known to us in his epistles. That the thought is at least differently presented in different epistles is clear. A generation ago most critics were confident that the differences could be explained by development through lapse of time. The idea of evolution seemed at that period to be the universal clue to knowledge in all fields, and the epistles were studied as documents for ' the evolution of Paulinism '. It may well be that this school overpressed the evidence in the interests of a neat scheme of development. In reaction against this, the modern tendency is to deny that the thought of Paul underwent any substantial development during the period covered by the extant epistles, and to explain the acknowledged differences as due merely to differences of aim, or to the different circumstances in which the epistles were written. The earliest of the extant epistles, it is pointed out, can hardly be dated much, if at all, before A.D. 50. At that time Paul was at least forty years old, probably older. He had been a Christian for fifteen years or more, a trained theologian before that, and an active Christian teacher for at least twelve years, probably longer. That was surely long enough (it is urged) for him to have thought out his theology, and it is unlikely that in middle age he made any such advances in thought as we should be able to recognize. The epistles, then, presuppose as a background a fairly complete system of thought, subject to no substantial change, though each one presents only a certain aspect of that system relevant to the particular church to which the epistle was directed, in the particular circumstances which called it forth.

Now we can hardly doubt that Paul, as an active and

experienced missionary, was clear enough about the main lines of his theology before his first extant epistle was written, and I should fully admit the caution that we must not assume that because he does not happen to mention a particular idea in a given epistle, he had not yet thought of it, or had given it up.   I should only deprecate any presumption at the outset that the mind of Paul is not likely to have developed in middle age.   Some men have their system of thought fixed by the time they are forty, and never afterwards seriously modify it.   Others are at that age just beginning to see their way to a system.   And we may recall that about A.D. 50 Paul entered upon a new phase of his missionary work.   He abandoned Antioch and the Levant, and made for Corinth and Ephesus, with Rome and even Spain as remoter goals ; he found a new set of friends ; and his missionary methods changed to meet new circumstances.   So much we know.   Would it be surprising if his thought took fresh turns ?

In the paper which precedes this I tried to show that the epistles, studied from a psychological point of view, afford evidence of changes in the apostle's own character and personal attitude to life.   The most important change, of course, is that which we call his conversion.   But it was not the last change.   In particular I showed reason to suppose that about the time when he wrote II Corinthians he underwent a significant spiritual experience which left its mark.   I now propose to examine some of the differences in his teaching which a study of the epistles admittedly reveals, and to inquire whether such differences can be correlated with this spiritual change in the apostle himself. If so, then there would be reason to suppose that they represent real development, and are not merely the result of the circumstances or the particular aim of the several epistles.

I. THE CHRONOLOGICAL ORDER OF THE PAULINE EPISTLES

For this purpose it is necessary to make some assumption regarding the chronological order of the epistles themselves. Fortunately four of them can be dated fairly precisely. For brevity I will give the dates in A.D.[1] A difference of a year or two in absolute chronology is possible in most cases, but the relative order is certain :

   I Thessalonians : A.D. 50 (spring).
   I Corinthians : A D. 57.
  II Corinthians : A.D. 57–8.
      Romans : A.D. 59 (spring).

II Thessalonians, if, as is probable, it is genuine, must be dated within a few weeks of I Thessalonians, possibly before it, more likely after it. The date of Galatians is greatly disputed. I will not discuss it here, but refer to Burton's discussion in the introduction to his edition of the epistle in the *International Critical Commentary*. His arguments seem to me to be convincing. His conclusion is that the letter was written not earlier than Paul's stay at Corinth (50–1), and not later than his visit to Macedonia and Achaia after the Ephesian period (57–9), but that the balance is in favour of its being written at Ephesus (54–7). The view that Galatians was written before I Thessalonians has no considerable amount of support except in this country. The Pastoral Epistles present a problem of their own.[2] That they are genuine in their present form I cannot persuade myself. That they contain genuine Pauline elements seems highly probable, but to isolate these elements, still more to find a place for them in the known life of Paul, is a

---

[1] The system of chronology adopted here is that which I have stated and briefly defended in the Oxford *Helps to the Study of the Bible*, 1931, pp. 195–7. It is substantially that of Edward Meyer, *Ursprung und Anfänge des Christentums*. (I would take this opportunity of correcting a *lapsus calami* in that article. It states that Paul was ' brought before Gallio in autumn 52 '. As the context shows, autumn 51 was intended.)

[2] The most convincing treatment, in my opinion, is by P. N. Harrison, *The Problem of the Pastoral Epistles*.

difficult and delicate problem, which in any case cannot be effectively tackled until prior questions regarding the other epistles have been in some measure settled. I will therefore leave the Pastorals out of account. There remain Ephesians, Philippians, Colossians and Philemon, the dating of which is a matter for discussion.

These epistles, assuming their authenticity, were written by Paul from prison. So much we know from internal evidence. But as Paul himself tells us that he had been frequently imprisoned before the time of II Corinthians,[1] and Acts records imprisonments at Cæsarea and at Rome after that time, the mere fact that they were written from prison does not by itself settle the date. From the fourth century to the nineteenth the prevailing and almost unquestioned view was that they were written during the imprisonment at Rome with which the record in Acts ends. The first departure from this view was the suggestion that one or more of them may have been written from Cæsarea during the two years when Paul was awaiting trial there. If this suggestion were accepted, it would not alter the relative chronology of the Pauline Corpus, for the Captivity Epistles would still be later than Romans, and would still represent (if we ignore the Pastoral Epistles) the latest known phase of Paul's literary activity. But of recent years a theory has been put forth, and has won a good deal of support, that these four epistles, or certain of them, were written during an unrecorded imprisonment at Ephesus. If this were so, they would fall into the same period with the Corinthian correspondence, and before Romans. Thus the bulk of Paul's surviving literary output would fall within three or four years—Romans, I and II Corinthians, Ephesians, Philippians, Colossians, Philemon, and probably Galatians. For the interpreter of Paul's thought, therefore, the epistles would be no longer landmarks in his course over some fourteen years, but in the main a reflection of his mind as it was at one particular brief period in a long career. For any study of his develop-

[1] II Cor. xi. 23.

ment it is obviously important to arrive at some conclusion on this question, and the Ephesian hypothesis demands careful investigation.

I should like to premise a few remarks on the principles and methods of such an investigation.

(1) If there were a tradition going back continuously to the earliest period, then that tradition would hold the field unless and until evidence clearly compelled us to abandon it. The burden of proof would definitely rest upon the innovator. In the present case, however, we cannot speak of such a tradition. It is true that the majority of our early evidence assumes that the captivity epistles were written from Rome, but there is very little of it, and it is not quite unanimous, nor does it go back to a period at which we could count upon our authorities having independent information on the point. The Roman attribution is in all probability a theory based upon a comparison of the Epistles with the Acts of the Apostles, a theory which by the fourth century had commended itself to all informed opinion as better than any other. But the Ephesian attribution is a theory similarly based, and it would hardly be denied that the scholar of the present day, with improved critical methods, though with no other materials to work upon, is in at least as good a position to judge such theories as the fathers of the fourth century. Thus it is a case of hypothesis against hypothesis.

(2) In one respect indeed the older view has an advantage. We *know* that Paul was imprisoned for at least two years at Rome, during which he had abundant time and opportunity for correspondence. We do not *know* that he was imprisoned at Ephesus, nor are we likely ever to know this, unless some further evidence should turn up—which is not very probable. The advocates of the new view, therefore, have the initial task of making it sufficiently probable that there was in fact an unrecorded imprisonment at Ephesus.

(3) The advocates of the Ephesian theory deprecate any appeal to the evidence of language or thought in

determining the relations of Paul's writings one to another. The problem, they insist, is a purely historical one, to be decided on the basis of the known facts of Paul's movements and those of his friends. It is only when we have determined the order of the epistles on such grounds that we can proceed to study their language and thought. Otherwise we introduce a subjective factor, and are in danger of a *circulus in probando*.

The danger no doubt exists ; but in determining the relations of ancient writings, we are often obliged to depend on just such considerations of language and thought. The arrangement of the Platonic dialogues, e.g. is necessarily based for the most part upon evidence of that kind, and used with a due sense of responsibility such evidence is entirely admissible. When, as in the case of Paul, we have the advantage of definite historical points to start from, then in framing the hypothesis regard should chiefly be paid to concrete recorded facts ; but when it comes to testing the hypothesis, similarity or dissimilarity of thought and language is a real factor in deciding whether two given writings are or are not likely to stand relatively close in time and circumstances to one another. And it may be urged that to suppose it possible to come to a conclusion solely on the basis of a comparison of the concrete historical data of the epistles on the one hand and the Acts on the other would be to underestimate the fragmentary character of both sources. The endless varieties of reconstructions of the facts which have been offered—and, I may add, are offered by advocates of the Ephesian hypothesis— show how far from complete our knowledge of the facts is and must remain. There are certainly cases where I should say that a recorded fact is of such uncertain interpretation that an argument based upon it is far more subjective than an argument derived from linguistic comparison. I shall, however, conduct the argument on the ground chosen by the advocates of Ephesus, up to the point at which the strictly historical evidence is exhausted.

(4) It would be useless and needless to state again the

generally accepted case for Rome, or to go over the familiar reconstruction of the facts of the closing years of Paul's life which presupposes that the captivity epistles belong to that period. Admittedly it is a reconstruction, and if the captivity epistles were shown to belong to another period it would largely fall to the ground. If, however, the Ephesian hypothesis fails to maintain itself, then we shall return to the view of Paul's later years which has seemed to most critics reasonable and probable, on the Roman hypothesis.

I proceed therefore to a consideration of the Ephesian hypothesis in comparison with the Roman. It must be some embarrassment to the advocates of that hypothesis, as it certainly is to their critics, that there are hardly two of them who hold it in the same form. Some put all the captivity epistles at Ephesus, some put Philippians there and the rest at Cæsarea or Rome, others put Philippians at Rome or Cæsarea and the rest at Ephesus. Some assume one imprisonment at Ephesus, others more than one. It will be simplest if instead of attempting to deal with the various and in part mutually contradictory forms of the hypothesis I select for treatment one of the most recent and elaborate presentations of it, and the only really thorough presentation of it in English, Professor George S. Duncan's book, *St. Paul's Ephesian Ministry* (Hodder & Stoughton, 1929).

Professor Duncan's thesis is that during the period covered by Acts xix. 1 – xx. 1 Paul was imprisoned three times, twice at Ephesus and once somewhere else in the Province of Asia, probably at Laodicea. The first of these imprisonments was before the writing of I Corinthians, and it was at this time that Philippians was written. The second was at the time of the riot at Ephesus, and at this time Paul wrote Colossians, Philemon and Ephesians. It is to be observed however, that Ephesians offers practically no independent historical data, so that for practical purposes we have to consider Colossians and Philemon alone for this second imprisonment. The question therefore of

G

the authenticity of Ephesians need not be discussed in this connection. The third imprisonment was after Paul had left Ephesus, and is the θλῖψις referred to at the beginning of II Corinthians.[1] This third imprisonment, however, does not greatly concern us, since it is arranged to accommodate some fragments of II Timothy, and we are leaving the Pastorals out of account.

We are now to examine the arguments by which Dr. Duncan arrives at this position.

1. Was Paul imprisoned at Ephesus?

First, he inquires what direct evidence there is to show that Paul was imprisoned at Ephesus. There is the direct statement of the apocryphal Acts of Paul, but on this he rightly lays little stress. He attaches more weight to the statement of the Marcionite Prologue to Colossians: ' apostolus jam ligatus scribit eis ab Epheso '. The value of this statement, however, is seriously weakened by the fact that these prologues ascribe Philemon, as well as ' Laodiceans ' (i.e. our Ephesians) to Rome. If there is one thing certain it is that Colossians and Philemon were written at the same time and place. Apart from this, he alleges no direct evidence that Paul was imprisoned at Ephesus. He proves only (a) that Paul was imprisoned more frequently than the author of Acts has recorded imprisonments ;[2] and (b) that the Ephesian ministry was much more troubled by opposition and persecution than Acts allows us to see.[3] So much is certain. It is therefore possible that Paul was imprisoned at Ephesus, and wrote letters from an Ephesian prison. But direct evidence for such an imprisonment can be forthcoming, as Duncan rightly urges, only from the captivity epistles themselves, on the hypothesis that they belong to Ephesus rather than to Rome. His task is to show that the Ephesian hypothesis meets the comparatively few known facts better than the

---

[1] II Cor. i. 8.
[2] II Cor. xi. 23 ; I Clem. v. 6.
[3] Evidence in I and II Cor. passim, and Rom. xvi.

Roman hypothesis. If he can convince us of that, then the evidence of the captivity epistles is available for the reconstruction of the Ephesian period.

2. Were the Captivity Epistles written from Rome?

It will be convenient to take first Dr. Duncan's arguments against the Roman hypothesis. First as regards Colossians and Philemon :

(i) Aristarchus (in Col. iv. 10) and Epaphras (in Philem. 23) are called Paul's ' fellow-prisoners ' (συναιχμάλωτοι). We have no evidence that either of them was imprisoned at Rome, and it is difficult to suppose that some fresh outbreak of hostility had occurred at Rome, which might have led to their arrest. On the other hand we have evidence in Acts that Aristarchus was actually apprehended at Ephesus, and it is not difficult to imagine that Epaphras also suffered in the same way.

But we observe that according to Acts,[1] when Aristarchus was apprehended, during the riot, Paul was not ; though on this point Duncan rejects the evidence of Acts, believing, without direct evidence, that Paul *was* arrested at this time. Further, according to Acts, Aristarchus set sail with Paul for Rome,[2] in some sort sharing his imprisonment. We are not told that he left the party at any point in the voyage, and to assume without authority that he separated from Paul at Myra is an irresponsible conjecture, even though it is supported by the great name of Lightfoot. We have therefore constructive evidence that Aristarchus was with Paul when he was imprisoned at Rome, and direct evidence that he was a prisoner at Ephesus but not a fellow-prisoner with Paul. For Epaphras there is no evidence one way or the other.[3]

---

[1] Acts xix. 29–30. [2] Acts xxvii. 2.

[3] It is by no means certain that the word συναιχμάλωτος as used by Paul necessarily means anything so definite as that the person in question was in the same prison at the same time with Paul through similar legal procedure. Some writers indeed hold that αἰχμάλωτος, meaning ' prisoner of war ', is not equivalent to δέσμιος, a person committed to gaol, and therefore implies nothing about imprisonment in the literal sense.

(ii) According to Colossians [1] and Philemon [2] Paul is surrounded by a group of friends. Only one of these (Luke) is definitely known to have been with him at Rome. Two of them (Aristarchus and Timothy) are known to have been with him at Ephesus, and others have connection with Ephesus or the Province of Asia.

It will be well to go over the list, premising however that if the captivity epistles are not Roman there is no source from which it is possible to learn who was or was not with Paul at Rome, apart from those who arrived there in his company according to Acts xxviii. 16.

Aristarchus : was with Paul at Ephesus, Acts xix, and accompanied him to Rome, on the natural reading of Acts xxvii–xxviii.

Epaphras of Colossæ : no evidence. Duncan argues it is more natural to find him at the neighbouring Ephesus than at the distant Rome. But wherever Paul was, if he was to keep in touch with his churches, somebody must make the journey, long or short.

Onesimus of Colossæ. See below.

Timothy : was with Paul at Ephesus (Acts xix. 22, and II Corinthians). No evidence that he was ever at Rome. But see below.

Mark : No evidence for either Ephesus or Rome. Duncan admits he probably did go to Rome, presumably on the evidence of 1 Peter.

Tychicus : of Asia, and therefore more likely to be at Ephesus than at Rome. But why? He travelled as a delegate to Jerusalem,[3] and if Paul, at Rome or elsewhere, was to be kept in touch with the churches of Asia, he was a natural intermediary.

Jesus Justus : no evidence for Ephesus or Rome.

---

[1] Col. i. 1—Timothy ;   iv. 10–14—Aristarchus, Mark, Jesus Justus, Epaphras, Luke, Demas.

[2] Philem. 1—Timothy ;   23–4—Epaphras, Mark, Aristarchus, Demas, Luke.

[3] Acts xx. 4.

Luke : certainly with Paul at Rome, Acts xxviii. 16.[1]
No evidence that he was ever at Ephesus, unless Colossians and Philemon were written there, though we may
think it probable.

Demas : no evidence for Ephesus or Rome.   Duncan
thinks that as he was a Macedonian he would be more
likely to be found at the neighbouring Ephesus than at
the distant Rome.   But see Epaphras and Tychicus.

Epaphroditus of Philippi : no evidence for Rome or
Ephesus.   Philippi is somewhat nearer Ephesus than
Rome ;   but see Demas, Epaphras, and Tychicus.

Now really, can this argument be taken seriously ?   We
have a list of ten people who were with Paul when he
wrote these letters.   Of these ten, we have certain evidence
of two at Ephesus and one at Rome, probable evidence
for one at Ephesus and two at Rome.   For six we have no
evidence one way or the other.   Four of the six lived at
places nearer to Ephesus than to Rome, but to argue that
therefore they were more likely to have been with Paul
there than at Rome is to misconceive the conditions of the
Pauline mission, which depended on the mobility of the
persons who either belonged to Paul's personal staff, like
Luke and Timothy, or acted as delegates of his churches,
like Tychicus.   The case of Onesimus I reserve.

Next, as regards Philippians :

(i) Philippians implies acute Jewish opposition.[2]   This
is attested for Ephesus by Acts.[3]   On the other hand,
Acts represents the Roman Jews as meeting Paul in a
friendly if cautious spirit, and saying that they know
nothing against him.[4]

Against this, we observe that the Jewish opposition of
which Paul speaks is at Philippi, and not necessarily at
Rome also, and that on the other hand even if Acts cor-
rectly represents the cautious neutrality of the Roman

[1] Assuming that he is the author of the ' Travel-diary ' from which the
' We '-passages of Acts are drawn.
[2] Phil. iii. 2–3.   [3] Acts xix. 9 ; xx. 19.   [4] Acts xxviii. 17–22.

Jews at the moment of Paul's arrival, it is a further step
to assume that when they knew more about him they still
refrained from hostility. In view of what took place at
other places, it is surely an improbable assumption.

(ii) Philippians also implies opposition from fellow-
Christians.[1] The speech at Miletus expresses apprehen-
sion of false teaching in the church at Ephesus,[2] and the
last chapter of Romans, which Duncan takes to be addressed to Ephesus, agrees with this.[3] I cannot accept this
view of Romans xvi for reasons which I have given elsewhere.[4] But there is no difficulty in believing that at
Ephesus, as at most places, Paul suffered from dissensions
in the Christian community.

But on the other hand, it is impossible to understand the
Epistle to the Romans unless we suppose that Paul had
good reason for thinking that his Gospel needed to be
defended before the Roman Christians, and that he expected opposition there. We may add that all we know
of Roman Christianity in the next age suggests that the
influence of Paul was never dominant in that church ; nor
was its theology of a definitely Pauline type.

If these are the only arguments that can be brought
against the Roman hypothesis, then it cannot be said to be
seriously shaken. Nevertheless, it may be that while there
is little against Rome, there are positive arguments in
favour of Ephesus, and since in both cases we are dealing
with nothing more than an hypothesis, the hypothesis
which explains the larger number of facts must prevail.
We turn therefore to Dr. Duncan's statement of reasons
for connecting the captivity epistles with Ephesus rather
than with Rome.

3. Were the Captivity Epistles written from Ephesus ?

First, then, as regards Colossians and Philemon.

(i) Onesimus is more likely to have fled to the neighbouring Ephesus than to the distant Rome.

---

[1] Phil. i. 15–18, iii. 18–19 (?).   [2] Acts xx. 29–30.   [3] Rom. xvi. 17–20.
[4] *The Moffatt Commentary* : Romans, pp. xvii–xxiv.

This seems plausible. But a moment's reflection may convince us that we are here talking of things about which we know nothing. We cannot know either what was in Onesimus' mind or what his opportunities for travel may have been. If we are to *surmise*, then it is as likely that the fugitive slave, his pockets lined at his master's expense, made for Rome *because* it was distant, as that he went to Ephesus because it was near. But this meeting of the runaway slave with the imprisoned apostle is in any case an enigma. Did he mean to go to Paul? Or was he taken to him? Or was it the long arm of coincidence that brought about such an improbable meeting? No secure argument can be based upon an incident which we cannot in any case explain.

(ii) Paul requests Philemon to provide a lodging for him.[1] When he was imprisoned at Rome, he had, so far as we know, no intention of returning to Asia. His intention had been to go on from Rome to Spain.[2]

This is a real point in favour of the Ephesian hypothesis. At the same time we do not know that Paul would have held to his intention in the greatly changed circumstances. Like all practical men, he was open to change his mind, as in fact we know both from Acts and from the Epistles he not infrequently did. On the Roman hypothesis, the emergence of the Colossian ' heresy ' may well have led Paul to plan a visit to Asia before setting out on further travels, whether or not the plan was ever fulfilled.

(iii) Colossians gives the impression that the Christianity of Colossæ was of recent origin, and is therefore more likely to have been written within three years of the founding of the Church there than some ten years later.

This is an entirely subjective argument. No doubt Colossian Christianity was of comparatively recent foundation, but I can find nothing in the epistle to suggest that it was two years rather than twelve years old.

(iv) When Paul wrote Colossians and Philemon (though not when he wrote Ephesians, apparently), Timothy was

[1] Philem. 22.   [2] Rom. xv. 22–4.

with him. We have no evidence that Timothy was ever in Rome.

A sound point, so far as it goes. But where probability must play so large a part in the argument, the advocates of Rome are entitled to reply that it is on all grounds *probable* that Paul's chief lieutenant visited Rome some time or other while Paul was there. The rest of Duncan's elaborate discussion of the movements of Paul and Timothy during the Ephesian period is of importance only if it be granted that a place for the epistles must be found in this period. It shows clearly enough that if this be granted, these movements offer no difficulty. It is not relevant to the question whether Ephesus is a more likely place than Rome for the writing of the epistles.

As regards Philippians, two of the arguments relating to Colossians and Philemon are again in place :

(i) Timothy is present.

(ii) Paul is contemplating a visit to Philippi.[1] This argument is slightly stronger for Philippians than for Colossians and Philemon, since we know that when Paul was at Ephesus he was contemplating a visit to Macedonia,[2] whereas, so far as we know, he intended to proceed from Rome to Spain. But once again, it is possible that Paul changed his mind. The Epistle to the Romans shows that he depended for his proposed Spanish mission on the support of Rome. But on the Roman hypothesis, Philippians shows that a large section of the Roman church was opposed to him. We must consider the possibility that this fact might lead Paul, even if he was liberated from the Roman imprisonment, to postpone the Spanish journey, while the Jewish opposition at Philippi might make him feel that a visit to Macedonia was desirable.

But further,

(iii) Philippians implies a number of journeys between Philippi and Paul's place of imprisonment. While Paul had been in prison (*a*) news of him reached Philippi, (*b*) Epaphroditus was sent to him with a gift, (*c*) Epaphro-

[1] Phil. ii. 24.   [2] I Cor. xvi. 5-9.

ditus fell ill, and news of his illness reached Philippi, (d) Epaphroditus received news of the grief of the Philippians at his illness.   To these we may add certain prospective journeys : (e) Epaphroditus is to be sent with the letter to Philippi, (f) Timothy is to be sent to Philippi when occasion offers, (g) Timothy is to return and report, and finally (h) Paul hopes to visit Philippi if possible.   Now from Rome to Philippi is some 360 miles by land to Brindisi, a day's voyage across the Adriatic, and some 370 miles along the Via Egnatia.   From Ephesus to Philippi was only from six to ten days in all.   From which point are all these journeys likely to have been undertaken ? Surely from Ephesus.

Prima facie a good argument, the strongest there is in favour of attributing Philippians to Ephesus.   But it is to be observed that while an Ephesian imprisonment can only have lasted a few weeks at most, in adopting the Roman hypothesis we are dealing with an imprisonment of at least two years, allowing ample time for all these journeys.   On that hypothesis, assuming that the Philippians wanted to send a gift to Paul, and that Epaphroditus fell ill at an inconvenient moment, how were these long journeys to be avoided ? [1]

(iv) The gift of the Philippians and its acknowledgment raises some difficulties.   Paul thanks the Philippians for having at long last (ἤδη ποτέ) thought of him.   He corrects himself : of course they had thought of him before, but had no opportunity to send a gift.[2]   Suppose Paul is at Rome.   Then apparently it was twelve years or more since he had received anything from them.[3]   Would it

---

[1] Josef Schmid, *Zeit und Ort der paulinischen Gefangenschaftsbriefe*, pp. 78–90, reckons that journeys (a)–(d) could be carried out between Rome and Philippi within five or six months, allowing for two or three weeks to collect the money to send to Paul, and for some small intervals between the journeys ; but that the time might be considerably reduced if news that Paul had started for Rome reached Philippi while he was still on the way.   Since he lost a whole winter in Malta, it is conceivable that Epaphroditus reached Rome as soon as Paul himself.

[2] Phil. iv. 10.

[3] Viz. at Thessalonica (Phil. iv. 16), and possibly at Corinth (II Cor. xi. 8).

not amount to a cutting piece of irony to suggest that in all
that time they had had no opportunity of contributing to
his needs—especially considering that he had visited
Philippi twice in the meantime ?   If, on the other hand,
he is writing from Ephesus, before the date of I Corinthians,
then the interval is perhaps no more than three or four
years, and during part of that time Paul had been in the
East or travelling in τὰ ἀνωτερικὰ μέρη, so that opportunity
may really have been lacking.

This looks like a strong argument.   But let us consider
what we know of the financial position during the Ephesian
period.   At that time Paul was raising his relief fund for
Jerusalem.[1]   Dr. Duncan indeed holds that he did not start
appealing to Macedonia for this fund until after the date
which he assigns to Philippians.   That I think improbable,
but let us grant it.   At least he was at this very time pressing the appeal at Corinth.   The appeal gave to his enemies
there an awkward handle for a charge of πλεονεξία.[2]   He
was, they said, really collecting money for himself.   How
damaging it would have been if at this very moment he
was known to be accepting gifts of money for himself from
the Philippians in the neighbouring province, without saying anything to them about the relief fund !   And as for
opportunity, he tells us that the Macedonian churches
were at this time suffering from grave economic depression.
Out of their ' deep poverty ' they contributed to the
fund.[3]   How long the depression lasted we cannot say, but
at least until the collection was finished Paul might have
said to the Philippians ἐφρονεῖτε, ἠκαιρεῖσθε δέ—' you
had the mind, but lacked the opportunity '.   Thus this
argument recoils upon its author.   The one time when
Paul was least likely to have received a gift of money from
Philippi was the Ephesian period.

(v) Phil. i. 30, τὸν αὐτὸν ἀγῶνα ἔχοντες οἷον εἴδετε ἐν
ἐμοὶ καὶ νῦν ἀκούετε ἐν ἐμοί—' you have the same conflict
as you saw me having and now hear of me having '.   This
(it is said) is more natural if the ' conflict ' of Paul which

---

[1] I Cor. xvi.   [2] II Cor. xii. 14–19.   [3] II Cor. viii. 1–6.

the Philippians saw (his imprisonment at Philippi) was near in time to the ' conflict' of which they heard (his imprisonment at Ephesus).

I can see no force in this argument.

To sum up this stage of the investigation : for Colossians and Philemon, argument (iii) may be wiped out ; argument (iv)—the presence of Timothy—is valid but has small weight ; arguments (i) and (ii)—Onesimus and the lodging at Colossæ—have *prima facie* weight, but are inconclusive ; for Philippians, arguments (iv) and (v) may be wiped out ; argument (i)—the presence of Timothy—is valid but has small weight ; argument (ii)—the proposed visit to Philippi—has *prima facie* weight, but is inconclusive ; argument (iii)—the length and frequency of the journeys—is valid, but loses much of its weight if we recognize that wherever Paul may have been at the time, circumstances compelled frequent intercommunication with Philippi, and if Ephesus was near, the Roman imprisonment was long.

It must be observed that since on Dr. Duncan's hypothesis these epistles were not written during one and the same imprisonment, the arguments affecting them severally do not form a cumulative series. We could accept the Ephesian origin of Philippians without any resultant presumption in favour of the Ephesian origin of Colossians and Philemon, and *vice versa.*

The net result so far is that the Ephesian hypothesis has some small advantage in each case, provided we are at liberty to assume that Paul was imprisoned at Ephesus. But so far we have only been convinced that such an imprisonment is possible. Unless it can be shown to be probable, then the advantage after all would lie with the Roman hypothesis, since we know that Paul was imprisoned at Rome.

4. Do the Captivity Epistles refer to Imprisonment at Ephesus?

Dr. Duncan's proof, briefly, runs as follows. A comparison of Acts and the epistles to the Corinthians shows that there were three acute crises during the Ephesian period. Granted that a *prima facie* case had been made out for connecting the captivity epistles with Ephesus, it is now legitimate to correlate their evidence with that of Acts and I and II Corinthians. By a close examination of all the data of the captivity epistles, it is shown that the *data* of Philippians would be consistent with an imprisonment at the time of the first crisis, and the *data* of Colossians and Philemon with an imprisonment at the time of the second crisis. For evidence of an imprisonment at the time of the third crisis we must turn to II Timothy, which lies outside our present field. It is not necessary to follow the minute examination of the *data* of the captivity epistles, unless we have first convinced ourselves that the *data* of Acts and I and II Corinthians are consistent, as Dr. Duncan avers, with two imprisonments at the times indicated.

(i) The first crisis is referred to in I Cor. xv. 30-32 : τί καὶ ἡμεῖς κινδυνεύομεν πᾶσαν ὥραν ; καθ᾽ ἡμέραν ἀποθνήσκω . . . εἰ κατ᾽ ἄνθρωπον ἐθηριομάχησα ἐν Ἐφέσῳ, τί μοι τὸ ὄφελος ; (as the argument partly turns on the meaning of the Greek, I reserve the translation of these words). That Paul is referring to a severe crisis of opposition cannot be doubted. The question is whether his expressions suggest an imprisonment. Paul is not at the moment of writing in prison, for he is free to arrange his movements. Thus the ' hourly peril ', the ' daily death '—strong expressions enough,—have no connection with an imprisonment. The only question is that of the meaning of εἰ κατ᾽ ἄνθρωπον ἐθηριομάχησα. The fight with beasts, Duncan thinks, must be literal. But, he goes on, it is impossible that Paul actually fought with beasts in the arena, for in that case under Roman law he would have lost his citizen rights, which we know he retained. The meaning therefore must

be ' if I had fought with beasts (as in fact I did not) '.
Paul therefore was in such a position that he might have
been condemned to fight with beasts, though actually he
escaped that fate.   Therefore, he had been on trial for
his life, and no doubt during or preceding the trial he was
imprisoned.

This is acute and ingenious.   But there are difficulties.
The condemnation of a Roman citizen to the beasts was an
exceptional thing, reserved, so far as our information goes,
for murderers, especially parricides, and for rebels.[1]   No
doubt at a later date, when Christianity was outlawed,
Christians might be treated as rebels, but even then, we
learn that in the persecution at Lyons and Vienne,[2] while
non-citizens were condemned to the beasts, Roman citizens
were sentenced to be beheaded, though it is true that one
of them was in the end unconstitutionally sent to the arena
at the urgency of the mob.   But there is no evidence to
suggest that before the Neronian persecution such a sentence on a Christian who was a Roman citizen could be
seriously contemplated.   It is unthinkable that such a
penalty should have been proposed for the offence with
which Duncan, on very slender evidence, supposes Paul
to have been charged, viz, constructive ' temple-robbery '
(ἱεροσυλία) consisting in the alleged diversion of the contributions of Christian Jews from the Temple at Jerusalem
to his own relief fund.   If the cry ' Ad leonem ! ' was raised
against Paul at all, it was surely no more than an irresponsible outburst of popular fury.   But in that case it affords
no evidence for an imprisonment, since such an outburst
might well have taken place at any public gathering (like,
for example, the assembly in the theatre at the time of the
riot).   Thus even if ἐθηριομάχησα is taken literally, and not,
as seems more likely, metaphorically, it does not support
the theory that Paul was imprisoned at this time.

A further difficulty is the silence of Acts on the supposed

[1] For the legal aspect of the matter, see Schmid, *Zeit und Ort*,
pp. 51 *sqq.*
[2] Euseb., *H.E.* V. i.

imprisonment.   This is not in itself a very serious difficulty.
Whether or not Paul was imprisoned at this time, he certainly had to face bitter opposition, of which Acts says
nothing.[1]   In any case Luke does not seem to have been
present at the time.   But it is nevertheless somewhat difficult to understand why he has suppressed any reference
to a trial which ended in acquittal, as we know must have
been the case, if there was a trial at all, since Paul was at
liberty when he wrote I Corinthians.   Dr. Duncan accounts
for this by unearthing an interesting fact which had not,
I think, been noticed previously.   The proconsul at the
time, who must have tried Paul, and also must have
acquitted him, was M. Junius Silanus.   This Silanus was
murdered by Agrippina's orders in A.D. 54, because he was
feared as a possible pretender to the imperial throne.   Now
Acts was written, according to Dr. Duncan, as an apology
for Paul when he was on trial at Rome.   It would have
been bad tactics to claim for Paul that he had found a
friend in Cæsar's enemy.   Luke therefore simply passed
over the whole episode.

This is ingenious, and on the assumption that Paul's
Roman imprisonment fell in the years 60–62, and that Acts
was written at that time in order to assist in his defence, it
would account for the silence of Acts.   But although such
an early date for Acts has found occasional support since
it was first propounded in 1855, the majority of critics, for
reasons which seem to me entirely cogent, though they
cannot be discussed here, assign it to a much later period.
Harnack's limits, 78–93, would be accepted by most critics,
apart from those who would push the composition of the
book into the second century.   But by A.D. 78 the fact
that the proconsul of Asia had been a victim of Nero
would certainly not prejudice the reputation of one who
had received favour from him, and we can only remain
astonished that Luke, even though he was not an eye-
witness of Paul's triumphant acquittal, failed to add it to

---

[1] Acts xix. 9 apparently refers to an earlier part of the Ephesian
ministry.

his other instances of the favourable attitude of the imperial authorities.[1]

In spite of the silence of Acts, however, we cannot absolutely rule out the possibility that among the sufferings to which Paul alludes in I Corinthians imprisonment was included.   We have therefore to ask whether the imprisonment of Philippians would naturally fit in with his circumstances at that time.   In Philippians Paul faces the possibility, or even the probability, that his imprisonment will end in death.[2]   But in fact he, as a Roman citizen, was not in danger of suffering the extreme penalty as the immediate result of any sentence of a provincial court since he could always play his trump card, an appeal to Cæsar. Thus, in default of cogent evidence, we should not be prepared to admit that the situation presupposed in Philippians could have arisen at Ephesus at this time ; and, as we have seen, no such evidence is forthcoming.

The case therefore for placing Philippians during an imprisonment at Ephesus before the writing of I Corinthians breaks down, and in the course of the investigation we have found that it is difficult to place it anywhere else than in Rome, where alone Paul could fear that his imprisonment would end immediately in death.

(ii) We now turn to the second crisis at Ephesus, which Dr. Duncan places at the time of the riot raised by Demetrius.   Paul, he supposes, was placed in some kind of protective custody until the storm had blown over. During this ' imprisonment ' he supposes Paul to have written Colossians and Philemon (with Ephesians).   When he wrote these letters he was confidently expecting a speedy

[1] In my own view, following that of Edward Meyer (see *Helps to the Study of the Bible*, *loc. cit.*), Paul did not reach Rome before 62.   By that time Seneca, whose support, according to Duncan, Luke hoped to gain, was no longer in favour, and if Acts was composed with a view to the trial, we should have to ask why the reference to his brother Gallio was not suppressed for the same reasons as the reference to Silanus.

[2] That it is a ' life and death ' matter is clear from Phil. i. 20, and Paul's confidence that his life will be spared (i. 25) is not based on a calculation of probabilities, but on a conviction that his life is so important to his churches that he must escape, even though by a miracle.

release, and so far they would fit the hypothetical situation. But for this imprisonment no evidence at all is offered. It is not referred to in II Corinthians, for Duncan rightly sees that the θλῖψις of that epistle is something that happened after Paul's ' sorrowful visit ' to Corinth, which he places after the riot.   Nor is there any allusion to it in Acts.   And here the silence of Acts is even more surprising. For, if Colossians and Philemon were written at this time, then Luke was present, and he has in any case given an unusually full and vivid account of the riot, ending with the words, ' After the riot was over, Paul sent for his disciples, made an encouraging speech, and then took his leave and departed for Macedonia.' [1]   There is no place here for an imprisonment.   Nor is it a case of mere silence, for Luke relates that during the riot the crowd laid hands on Gaius and Aristarchus but that Paul was kept out of their way.[2]   The clear implication is that Paul was not molested on this occasion.   If in fact he was arrested and imprisoned, with however benevolent intentions, then the author of Acts has definitely misled his readers.   But if he was so negligent, or so dishonest, a reporter, then it is hazardous to rely upon his record, as Dr. Duncan does on other occasions, even down to details.   If Acts is to be trusted at all, there was no imprisonment at Ephesus at this time.   Suppose, however, we waive this point, and allow that Paul was put in protective custody at the instance perhaps of the friendly Asiarchs.   Then surely the pathos of the ' ambassador in bonds ' (Eph. vi. 20, Philem. 9) is overdone, if the writer knew that his ' imprisonment ' was a friendly device to save him from the violence of the mob.   After all, the letters do not fit the supposed situation.

The case, therefore, for an Ephesian origin of Colossians and Philemon (with Ephesians) does not so much break down as go by default.   There is no case to send to the jury.

We may sum up as follows.   (i) As regards Philippians : the Ephesian hypothesis was shown to have some small

---

[1] Acts xx. 1.   [2] Acts xix. 29–31.

balance of advantage over the Roman hypothesis on the score of the presence of Timothy, the great distance between Rome and Philippi, and the fact that we know Paul to have contemplated visiting Philippi from Ephesus, whereas we do not know that he thought of visiting it after his Roman imprisonment. But the bare possibility that the imprisonment of Philippians could be placed at Ephesus shortly before I Corinthians has changed on investigations to a definite improbability, verging on impossibility. The balance therefore tips definitely to the side of Rome. (ii) As regards Colossians and Philemon the Ephesian hypothesis was shown to have some slight balance of advantage over the Roman hypothesis, on the score that Timothy was present, that Onesimus was more likely to meet Paul at Ephesus than at Rome, and that Paul is more likely to have thought of visiting Colossæ from Ephesus than from Rome. In this case the bare possibility that these epistles were written during an imprisonment at the time of the riot remains a bare possibility, supported by no evidence, and confronted by the serious difficulty of charging the author of Acts with deliberate misrepresentation. This is enough to destroy the balance of advantage, and we must report something like a dead heat between the two hypotheses. But this being so, we are surely justified in recalling that we know that Paul was imprisoned at Rome, while it has not been made even definitely probable that he was imprisoned at Ephesus, and concluding that the net advantage after all rests, for these epistles also, with the Roman hypothesis, against which no serious arguments were adduced.

5. *Arguments from Thought and Language*

It is at this point that I should bring forward those arguments from thought and language which Dr. Duncan, in common with other advocates of the Ephesian hypothesis, deprecates. Such arguments are too long and detailed to be set forth here. I would however offer a few observations. First, if Dr. Duncan's view is accepted,

H

then about 80 per cent. of Paul's total surviving literary
output is brought into one period of not more than five
years,[1] during which the letters follow in rapid succession.
Consequently, no argument can be founded on the recur-
rence of ideas or expressions in epistles of this group.   Dr.
Duncan realizes this and though he points out a number of
parallels he lays no stress upon them for the purpose of his
argument.   It might indeed strengthen his case if he could
show that within this group I Corinthians and Philippians
on the one hand and II Corinthians and the remaining
captivity epistles on the other have marked similarities.
He makes no attempt to show this, and indeed it is obviously
not so.   But while no argument can be based on *similarities*
in this field, the difficulties raised by the striking *dissimi-
larities* between epistles *ex hypothesi* written nearly at the
same time cannot be ignored.   The *data* on which the
Tübingen School founded their case against the authenticity of the captivity epistles are still facts.   No one can
deny that the style, vocabulary, and ideas of *Colossians* and
Ephesians, and to a less degree *Philippians*, show remarkable
differences from those of I and II Corinthians and Romans.
We may put the matter in this way : among the epistles
which the new theory assigns to the period between Paul's
arrival at Ephesus (Acts xix. 1) and his departure for
Jerusalem (Acts xx. 1), those which mention an imprisonment are also those which, as compared with all the other
Pauline Epistles, show the most striking peculiarities of
thought and diction.   If we had no life of Paul to guide us,
who can doubt that on this double ground these epistles
would have been regarded as forming a separate group
within the corpus of his writings, and conjecturally assigned
to a later period.   But seeing that we have a life of Paul,

---

[1] Reckoning from the earliest date for Galatians which is at all probable,
viz. the beginning of the Ephesian ministry, A.D. 54 in my chronology.   If
Galatians is later than I Corinthians, as I think probable, the period is less
than three years.   In reckoning the percentage, I have counted in the whole
of the Pastorals.   If, as I think, the Pastorals are mostly non-Pauline, the
percentage is greater.   If Galatians belongs to an earlier period, then the
percentage is still as high as 72 per cent., including the Pastorals.

if only a fragmentary one, and that this life gives us no imprisonment at the time of I and II Corinthians, but does give us an imprisonment some years later, we are entitled to allow full weight to the evidence of language and thought, and to prefer the later date.   The best hypothesis is that which accounts for the largest number of relevant known facts. Among the facts of the life of Paul, the external facts of journeys and imprisonments are not more relevant or important than the internal facts of his spiritual and intellectual life, as reflected in the varieties of thought and diction revealed in the epistles.

I have not raised here the question of the authenticity of these epistles.   Dr. Duncan accepts them all as Pauline. Few critics now have any serious doubts about Philippians, or about Philemon.   A majority would be prepared to accept Colossians.   Ephesians still lies under suspicion though many would accept it.   But the rehabilitation of these epistles has depended largely upon the Roman hypothesis, which allows a lapse of time to account for their peculiarities.   If the Roman hypothesis were discredited, then the question would be reopened with a prejudice against Pauline authorship.   If that hypothesis stands, then all that has been said in recent years in favour of Pauline authorship has full weight.[1]

It may seem that I have dealt at disproportionate length with the question of the captivity epistles.   But the Ephesian hypothesis is the most serious challenge that has been offered to the generally accepted view of the chronological order of the Pauline corpus.   It has not, I think, been thoroughly discussed in English literature of the subject, but one meets with a widespread vague idea that there is ' something in it '.   This can lead only to a blurring of the outlines of our picture of Paul's career.   Either it is true, and we must adjust our view of Paul's career to it,

---

[1] I have briefly discussed the question of the authorship of Colossians, Philemon, and Ephesians in the *Abingdon Commentary*, concluding that we may without misgiving treat the two former as Pauline (assuming that they were written from Rome), and that for Ephesians the difficulties of non-Pauline authorship are at least as great as those of the traditional attribution.

or it is false.   If, as I have tried to show, it cannot stand critical examination, then we may with some confidence assume that the captivity epistles represent the latest stage of Paul's literary activity, as it is known to us.   The precise order of the epistles within the captivity group is a more delicate question which we need not here decide.   On the whole it seems probable that Philippians followed rather than preceded the others, but this view is not altogether without difficulties.

II. EVIDENCE OF DEVELOPMENT IN THE EPISTLES

Assuming then the chronological order of the epistles which I have tried to substantiate, I proceed to study certain aspects of Paul's thought with a view to showing that it developed in certain directions.

Our point of reference is II Corinthians, and the spiritual experience which, as I suggested in a previous lecture, is reflected in that epistle.   In chs. x–xiii we are watching the resolution of a conflict in the apostle's mind.   His anxious striving to excel, and his resentment at opposition, failure and humiliation (of which there is evidence also in other epistles) here break out in a long tirade of invective and indignant self-vindication.   But he pulls himself up to recall an experience in which he heard the Lord saying, ' My grace is enough for you, for strength reaches perfection in weakness.'   And this is his response : ' I consent to weaknesses, insults, necessities, persecutions and tribulations, for Christ's sake ; for it is when I am weak that I am strong.' [1]   In other words, he has accepted weakness, limitation, and humiliation ; he has withdrawn his claim upon life for power, predominance, and conspicuous success.[2]   He has become reconciled to experience.

I propose now to trace certain changes of attitude which seem to date from the same point in his career, in two departments of religious thought, viz. (1) eschatology and

---

[1] II Cor. xii. 8–10.
[2] I here summarize briefly what was said above, pp. 80–82.

the valuation of the natural order, and (2) the universality
of the Christian religion.

1. Eschatology and the Valuation of the Natural Order

It seems clear that Paul started with eschatological
beliefs of the type best represented by such Jewish writings
as the Book of Enoch, the Apocalypse of Baruch and the
Apocalypse of Ezra (II Esdras), especially the last-named.
The apocalyptists despaired of the present world-order
('This Age'), as being under the dominion of diabolic
powers, and looked for a new order ('The Age to Come'),
in which the sovereignty of God would be effectively manifested in a radical renewal of the whole universe. His
enemies would be destroyed, the righteous dead would be
raised to share in His triumph, and the elect still living
would be transfigured into bodies of glory, to inhabit the
new heavens and new earth. All this would come about
by a catastrophic divine intervention, marked by the
appearance of God's vicegerent, the Elect One, sometimes
called the Son of Man (or the Man), who would rule the
new world in everlasting righteousness.

When Paul became a Christian, his new beliefs were
fitted into this framework. The Age to Come, he held,
had already begun, with the resurrection of Christ. It
must shortly be consummated by His appearance in glory.
Thus he tells us that he had preached to the Thessalonians
that they 'should turn from idols to the living and true
God, and await His Son from heaven—Jesus, who is our
deliverer from the coming retribution'.[1] They would not
have long to wait. Although Paul had already waited at
least fifteen years since his conversion, yet in his earliest
letters he is still expecting the Advent almost immediately.
The Thessalonians indeed had understood him to say ' that
the Day of the Lord is already here '.[2] He had to correct
this impression. Before the Lord comes, ' the man of in-
iquity ', the Antichrist, must appear, and so far his appearance is delayed. Yet he is already secretly at work, and

[1] I Thess. i. 9–10. [2] II Thess. ii. 2.

the time cannot be long.[1] At any rate, Paul is certain that
he himself and the majority of his converts will be alive to
' meet the Lord in the air '.   Evidently he had expressed
himself at Thessalonica in such unqualified terms that his
converts had been seriously shaken by the death of some
of their number before the Advent, and he reassures them,
and himself, that such exceptional cases will not be at a
disadvantage because they have been thus temporarily
separated from the main body of those who await the Lord
from heaven.[2]

Some seven years later, in writing I Corinthians, Paul
still betrays his conviction that he and at least some of his
converts will be alive to meet the Lord.   ' We shall not all
fall asleep, but we shall all be changed. . . . For there
will be a trumpet-call, and the dead will rise immortal,
and *we* shall be changed.'[3]   The emphatic ' we ' shows
that Paul unquestioningly places himself among the sur-
vivors.   The Advent therefore is still expected within the
period of his reasonable expectation of life.   He is still
certain that ' the time is short '.[4]   At the same time there
is a slight change of emphasis.   Whereas in I Thessalonians
it is distinctly exceptional for a Christian to die before the
Advent, in I Corinthians he has to assure his readers that
not all Christians will die.   He himself, with others, will
survive to the Advent.

After I Corinthians we hear no more of that confident
expectation, so far at least as Paul himself is concerned.
On the contrary, in II Corinthians he has faced the fact
that it is possible or probable that he will ' go to stay with
the Lord ' through death.   His ' outward self ' is decaying,
but his ' inward self ' is being renewed, and he has a ' house
not made with hands, eternal in the heavens ' with which
(by a mixture of metaphors) he will be ' clothed ' when his
earthly ' tabernacle ' is dissolved.[5]   It is possible that when
he says ' Death works in us but life in you,'[6] he means that

[1] II Thess. ii. 3–7.   [2] I Thess. iv. 13–17.
[3] I Cor. xv. 51–2 : οἱ νεκροὶ and ἡμεῖς are antithetical terms.
[4] I Cor. vii. 29.   [5] II Cor. v. 1–4.   [6] II Cor. iv. 12.

though he will die, his readers will survive until the Advent. In any case, the Advent is no longer to be in his lifetime. It seems probable that the extreme danger of death in which he had recently stood [1] had helped to alter his outlook in this respect. Logically this should make no difference to his conviction that the Lord will soon come ; but psychologically, an event which lies beyond the limits of one's own reasonable expectation of life, and belongs therefore to the unknown future, in which years and centuries are alike, has ceased to be in any vital sense imminent. And we do in fact find that in subsequent epistles the thought of the imminence of the Advent retires into the background.

In Romans we have the one passage, xiii. 11–14, ' Our salvation is now nearer than it was when we became Christians. The night is advanced : the day has drawn near.' The whole passage echoes I Thess. v. 1–11 ; but a comparison of the two passages reveals an unmistakable change of tone. In the earlier epistle the tone is one of intense, almost excited, urgency. *At any moment* the Lord may be here. In the later the tone is (shall we say ?) that of an earnest preacher, but not that of the herald of an imminent catastrophe. And this change of tone is more remarkable when we observe that this is the only passage of the kind in the whole long epistle, and it is almost by way of an afterthought, appended when the main business of the epistle is complete. Throughout the great argument no appeal is made to the thought of the imminent Advent. Instead, we have a greater emphasis than ever before upon the idea that the Christian, having died and risen with Christ, is already living the life of the new age.[2] The consummation indeed is still awaited, but awaited without urgency, because the substance of our hope is a present possession.[3]

In the captivity epistles we miss even this remnant of Paul's earlier impatient expectation. In Colossians, the

[1] II Cor. i. 8–9.   [2] Rom. vi. 1–11 ; viii. 9–11.
[3] Rom. viii. 18–39.

close of the ethical exhortations, iv. 1, corresponds with the point in Romans at which the thought of the Advent is adduced as an ethical motive, but there is no passage here corresponding to Romans xiii. 11–14. Again, i. 23, which speaks of 'the Gospel hope', and iii. 4, which speaks of the manifestation of Christ and our manifestation with Him in glory, would be appropriate points at which to remind the Colossians that this great hope was shortly to be fulfilled ; but there is no such reminder. The case of Philippians is even more striking, just because Paul, standing face to face with death, has much to say of heavenly glory. ' We await a Saviour from heaven, our Lord Jesus Christ, who will transfigure our body of humiliation into the form of His body of glory.' [1] It is the old expectation, but no longer with the earlier insistence on the imminence of the change. The moral of it is that we should bear in mind that ' we are a colony of heaven, from which we await our Saviour '. That is, the eschatological expectation has come to be subordinated to the thought of the heavenly life (the life of the new age) lived here and now. The words of iv. 5, ' the Lord is near ', are often taken to be an isolated expression of the imminence of the Advent. But the context here is not eschatological, and the words are a reminiscence of Psalm cxlv. 18, ' The Lord is nigh unto all them that call upon Him,' which speaks, as does the passage in Philippians, of the nearness of the Lord to hear and answer prayer. In Ephesians there is no passage which even approaches the thought of an imminent Advent.

We seem then to be able to trace a quite definite change of outlook on this particular point. It might perhaps seem that it is not of great importance, as being merely a readjustment, so to speak, of the eschatological time-table. But in effect it is much more than that. If the Advent is expected within a few years or months—or indeed at any moment—then the present life, with all its blessings and obligations, is strictly provisional, and the mind is set wholly upon glories to come. But if the Advent is deferred to

[1] Phil. iii. 20–1.

an indefinite future, then the present gains in significance. And as we have seen, side by side with a diminishing emphasis on the imminence of the Advent goes a growing emphasis on the eternal life here and now in communion with Christ. This is sometimes described as the trans-formation of eschatology into mysticism, and the expression will serve. Paul's thought was indeed never wholly eschatological nor did it ever become purely mystical, but there is nevertheless a real development, and it is note-worthy that the turning-point seems to lie somewhere about the time of II Corinthians.

There is a further consequent development with which I must deal more fully. Apocalyptic eschatology, as we have seen, implies a radical devaluation of the present world-order in all its aspects. The apocalyptists are never more eloquent than when they are describing the entire worthlessness of ' This Age ' and of the world and human life under its conditions. The only hope of good lies in the speedy passing away of the whole empirical order.

In Paul's earlier epistles a similar depreciation of the present order is evident. The clearest passage is I Cor. vii. The whole discussion of ethical problems in this chapter is controlled by the maxim : ' The time is short . . . the fashion of this world is passing away.' [1] The Christian therefore must detach himself from its transient concerns. Its joys and sorrows do not touch him. If he buys, it is not to possess. If he has a wife, let him be as though he had none. [2] The married man cares for the things of the world, the unmarried for the things of the Lord. [3] Detach-ment is best secured by refusing to take any interest in changing one's condition, but just ' carrying on ' until the end—if you are married, stay so, if unmarried, do not seek a wife, if a slave, never mind. [4] This doctrine of

---

[1] I Cor. vii. 29, 31.   [2] I Cor. vii. 29–31.   [3] I Cor. vii. 32–34.
[4] I Cor. vii. 27, 21. Here, however, there is a slight concession for εἰ καὶ δύνασαι ἐλεύθερος γενέσθαι μᾶλλον χρῆσαι almost certainly means ' If you do get a chance to be free, take advantage of it.' (See my article in *Journal of Theological Studies*, 1924, vol. xxvi, no. 101, p. 77.) The slave is not to set his heart on freedom : that would be ' caring for the things of the world ' ;

' carrying on ' may be regarded as some sort of mitigation
of the extreme other-worldliness which would withdraw
from the world altogether, but it is not due to any admission
of the worth of the natural order, but to Paul's robust
common sense, which similarly deprecated the tendency
of the Thessalonians to give up their employment and wait
for the end. The world may be coming to an end, but
while it lasts you must eat, and in order to eat you must
work.[1] But in the ethical passages of the Thessalonian
epistles there is no recognition of any positive value in
human institutions, any more than there is in I Corinthians.

It is therefore striking to find in Rom. xiii. 1–10, a positive valuation of the political institutions of the Roman
Empire. It is not simply a recognition that the worldly
power is there by God's ordinance. The apocalyptists
could say as much. Nor is it simply that the Empire is
there to restrain the final outburst of evil until the time
appointed by God for the appearance of Antichrist, as
Paul held when he wrote II Thessalonians. He now holds
that the Empire is a positively good thing. Its magistrates
are ' servants of God ', even ' priests of God ' (λειτουργοὶ
Θεοῦ), charged with a beneficent function in the providen-
tial government of the universe. We may contrast the
contemptuous tone in which the imperial courts of justice
are dismissed in I Cor. vi. 1–11. Thus to pay taxes is
not merely a counsel of prudence, nor even a meritorious
submission to human oppression, but a part of the service
of God and a way of fulfilling the command to love your
neighbour as yourself. The sharp distinction between ' the
things of the Lord ' and ' the things of the world ' has
begun to wear thin.

but if the opportunity comes his way he should not reject it.   Inconsistent,
perhaps, but hardly more so than the exhortation to the Thessalonians to
work.
[1] II Thess. iii. 6–12. Paul has learned from the ill-fated experiment in
Communism in the Church of Jerusalem. See my article ' Communism
in the N.T.', *Interpreter*, 1921, vol. xviii, no. 1. We must remember that
he had already had several years of missionary experience, which corrected
the severe logic of his eschatology.

Along with this recognition of the value of human institutions we may place the recognition of the instinctive goodness of the natural man in Rom. ii. 14-15 :

When pagans who have no law do by nature what the law enjoins, then, though they have no law, they are their own law, since they exhibit the effect of the law inscribed on their hearts, while their conscience bears witness, and their reasonings reciprocally condemn or defend them.

We may contrast this passage with the stern dualism of II Cor. vi. 14-vii. 1 (probably an erratic block from an earlier letter to Corinth of which the rest has been lost) : ' What participation has right with wrong, or what has light in common with darkness, or what agreement has Christ with Belial, or what part has a believer with an infidel ? '   Surely we have here again evidence of the new valuation of ' the world ' which went along with Paul's revision of eschatology.   We find the same attitude in the famous passage, Phil. iv. 8-9, where the expression is, with evident intent, made wide enough to cover ' virtue ' and ' praise ' wherever they are to be found—surely not in the Church alone.

It is noteworthy that the language and ideas of all these passages are reminiscent of Stoicism.   The new orientation of Paul's thought seems to have given him greater freedom to appreciate and appropriate the best elements in the loftiest moral philosophy of the pagan world.

In Colossians we find a still more remarkable development.   This is the first letter which contains a section dealing with Christian ethics in family life.[1]   It is not always realized how significant it is that there should be such a section at all.   In I Cor. vii. family life belongs to ' the things of the world ' as opposed to ' the things of the Lord '. It is a part of ' the fashion of this world ' which ' is passing away '.   All that Paul can say at that stage is ' Let those who have wives be as though they had none.'   On such

---

[1] Col. iii. 18–iv. 1.

a basis there could be no such thing as the Christianizing of family relationships. In Colossians we have a meagre enough treatment of family duties, but so far as it goes it is positive. 'Wives, be subject to your husbands, as is fitting *in the Lord.*' It is those last words that are important : marriage is now 'in the Lord'; it belongs to 'the things of the Lord'. 'Husbands, love your wives'—not, behave as though you had none.[1] 'Children obey your parents in all things, for this is pleasing *in the Lord.*' And children have their rights : 'Fathers, do not irritate your children, lest they should lose heart.' Slaves (who are also members of the *familia*) must render their service 'as to the Lord and not to men', and their masters must treat them with 'justice and equity'. Slaves are told 'You are the Lord's slaves,' and masters, 'You have a Master in Heaven.' Thus the slave, remaining in servitude within the social framework of the time, becomes 'in the Lord' a full moral personality, responsible directly to God, like his master. We may wish, from our modern point of view, that Paul had gone further ; but to take slavery in hand and set out to Christianize it was a more hopeful way of dealing with it than the complete detachment of I Cor. vii.

Here again the Stoic affinities of Paul's teaching are to be observed. The exposition of tables of duties (τὰ καθήκοντα [2]) under headings of this kind is characteristic of the popular teaching of that school. Hierocles the Stoic in the early second century arranged his work on social ethics in the following sections : (i) How to behave to the gods ; (ii) How to behave to one's country ; (iii) How to behave to parents ; (iv) On love between brothers ; (v) How to behave to kinsfolk ; (vi) Household management ;

---

[1] Is it a truism that husbands should love their wives? It was not so to all Greeks. See the pseudo-Demosthenic *Contra Neæram*, § 122, p. 1386 : 'We have courtezans for pleasure, concubines for the daily care of the body, and wives for the sake of having legitimate children and a trustworthy caretaker of the home.' Besides which, ἀγάπη is not ἔρως.

[2] This Stoic term reappears in Rom. i. 28, ποιεῖν τὰ μὴ καθήκοντα : cf. Col. iii. 18, ὡς ἀνῆκεν ἐν κυρίῳ.

(vii) On marriage and children.[1]   Hierocles certainly did
not originate this method.   There were doubtless Stoic
models for Paul in the first century.   But while he follows
the customary forms, the content of his teaching, slight as
it is, is something more than a mere adaptation of current
ethics.   The religious principle that in Christ there is no
distinction of male and female, bond and free, has begun
to find expression in social morality.   The woman, the
child, and the slave, while retaining their various degrees
of subordination according to the social structure of Græco-
Roman civilization, have claims as well as duties of their
own as moral personalities.

In Ephesians we have a still more remarkable development of the teaching on marriage (v. 21–33).   Here the
love of husband and wife becomes a sacramental symbol,
of the love of Christ and the Church.   That is to say, the
marriage relation, which in I Cor. vii. was regarded as
irrelevant to the Christian life, is made the vehicle of the
highest conceivable spiritual values.   It is clearly impossible at the same time to follow the two maxims :   ' Let
those who have wives be as though they had none,' and
' Love your wives as Christ loved the Church and gave
Himself up for it.'   This radical contradiction has been
taken as one reason for denying the Pauline authorship of
this epistle.   But it lies on the line of development which
we have traced.   The teaching of Ephesians fits into the
framework of Colossians, though it does not fit into the
framework of I Corinthians.   If the thought of Paul did
not change or develop, then it is impossible to attribute
Ephesians to him ; but it is only a little less impossible to
attribute Colossians to him, for the decisive difference lies
between I Corinthians and Colossians, not between Colossians and Ephesians.   If we are prepared to recognize a
development, then the teaching of Ephesians represents
on this side the climax of that development.

---

[1] Τίνα τρόπον θεοῖς χρηστέον, πῶς πατρίδι χρηστέον, πῶς χρηστέον τοῖς γονεῦσιν,
περὶ φιλαδελφίας, πῶς συγγενέσι χρηστέον, οἰκονομικός, περὶ γάμου καὶ παιδοποιίας.
See Prächter, *Hierokles der Stoiker.*   The text of Hierocles is reconstructed
from extensive excerpts in Stobaeus.

Once again therefore we have to report that while the earlier epistles show a radical denial of the value of the present order, the later epistles show a recognition of natural human goodness, of the relative value of human institutions, and of the possibility of taking them up into the Christian life.   The turning point is somewhere about the time of II Corinthians.

2. *Universalism, and the Idea of Reconciliation*

I tried above (pp. 72–74) to show that what we may call the Gentile question must have been already a factor in Paul's personal conflict before his conversion. The Pharisees in general were deeply concerned about the Gentiles. Many of them were active in proselytism. Their views regarding the ultimate fate of Gentiles varied through a wide range,[1] but a strong interest in the question seems to have been general.   For Paul the problem must surely have been pressing, with his natural sympathy and curiosity, and his upbringing in a great centre of pagan culture.   What his actual attitude was, whether that of the humaner and more broad-minded Pharisees, or that of the more narrow and gloomy school, we have no direct evidence to show.   But all that we can deduce of his general position—his fanatical strictness about the law, his intense nationalism, his gloomy intolerance, would suggest that he repressed all humaner tendencies in the interests of his legal absolutism.

It would seem that the Jewish writing which best represents Paul's pre-Christian position is the Apocalypse of Ezra (II Esdras). Again and again we find that this work raises the questions which Paul's Christian theology answers. A striking example is the question of faith and works in relation to the mercy of God and the salvation of men (viii. 32–36). The problem which most burdens the mind of ' Ezra ' is that of the fate of the majority of the human race. On his premises—that God has promised eternal life to those who keep His commandments, and to

---

[1] *Vide* G. F. Moore, *Judaism*, part II, chs. i, vii.

them alone—it follows inevitably that the great bulk of humanity has been created only to perish. In various forms the apocalyptist returns to the problem, and the divine voice inexorably confirms the revolting conclusion. While his human heart protests ' *O tu terra, quid peperisti . . . melius enim erat et ipsum pulverem non esse natum* ' (vii. 62 *sqq.*), the calm voice of the Judge of all coldly asserts and reasserts that as the earth produces but little gold and silver, and much base metal and clay ; as but little of the seed sown in it ever comes to maturity ; so it is eternally fitting that of mankind but a small remnant should be saved. ' *Ecce paene omnes in perditionem ambulant et in exterminium fit multitudo eorum* ' (x. 10).

I cannot but think that this same dreadful conflict raged in Paul's mind between his human feelings and the demands of that devotion to the Law in which he sought the glory of life. ' Ezra ' finds no way out : he steels his heart to accept this inflexible and gloomy eschatology in which at most but an elect handful of Jews inherits the Age to Come, while the rest of mankind perish in inconceivable misery. Paul did find a way out. In that very experience through which he himself died and rose again there was given the belief that not those who do the works of the Law are justified, but those who having no good works receive through faith the mercy of God (the belief which ' Ezra ' had suggested only, as it seems, to reject it, viii. 36) ; consequently the world to come could not be confined to Israel. From the very outset Paul's Christianity must have involved a mission to the Gentiles. It is true that we have no direct evidence in his epistles for the earliest years of his Christian life and doubt has been cast on the narrative in Acts,[1] on the ground that the story of the mission from Antioch is inconsistent with the statement that Paul's conversion included a call to preach to the Gentiles. In any case,

---

[1] Acts ix. 15, xxii. 21, xxvi. 16–18. It is to be observed that all three accounts of Paul's conversion represent it as being at the same time a call to preach to the Gentiles. This is more impressive if, as it seems reasonable to suppose, the various accounts go back to more than one source.

as soon as the evidence of epistles begins, Paul is a mission-ary to the Gentiles. The earliest of the epistles, I Thessa-lonians (A.D. 50) assumes, without arguing it, that the divine election has passed from the Jews to a church of Jews and Gentiles. Further, Gal. ii. provides evidence that in the period before his concordat with the Jerusalem apostles (probably A.D. 48), he had made uncircumcized Gentile converts ; and the implication of the whole passage is that he was not aware of this being any new departure. It was the kind of work he had begun in Syria and Cilicia fourteen years earlier. This evidence is indeed not con-clusive, but so far as it goes it confirms what I have shown to be extremely probable *a priori*, that for Paul to accept Jesus meant that he was outside the Law, and therefore on common ground with Gentiles, and hence that the true Church of Christ must rest upon the principle—' there is no distinction ' ; ' in Christ there is neither Jew nor Greek '.[1]

In one sense this already means the universality of the Christian religion. Yet we must define more closely what Paul's new position is. According to I Thess. ii. 16, ' the Wrath ' has fallen *finally* on the Jews,—εἰς τέλος implying that this sentence of reprobation cannot ever be reversed. Similarly, according to Gal. vi. 15–16, the Israel of God is co-extensive with those who believe in Christ and ex-cludes all those who make circumcision and the Law necessary to salvation. Unless he has expressed himself incautiously in the heat of controversy, not only Jews, but even Jewish Christians who enforce the Law are ' ana-thema ' (i.e. חֵרֶם, placed outside the holy community and devoted to ' wrath ', Gal. i. 8–9). The Law itself is not divine, but originates with those lower powers which are for Paul at least potentially the enemies of men's salvation —the angels in Jewish language, the ' elementals of the universe ' (στοιχεῖα τοῦ κόσμου) in pagan phrase.[2] To be

---

[1] Rom. iii. 22, x. 12 ; Gal. iii. 28 ; Col. iii. 11.

[2] Gal. iii. 19, iv. 8–11. As the Galatians are tempted to revert to Jewish usages, it can only be the observance of the Mosaic Law that is meant

committed to the Law is to fall under this domination, and outside the sphere of grace and election. On the other hand, all pagans are, of course, *ipso facto* outside the Israel of God, which can have no intercourse with them (II Cor. vi. 14–vii. 1).

Thus in place of the tiny remnant of Israel which alone will inherit life according to 'Ezra', Paul has put an equally closed and scarcely larger body of Christians, whether of Jewish or pagan origin, who repudiate the Law as a means of salvation.[1] His attitude to all who fall outside this small body is as negative as that of 'Ezra'. He is still content with the eschatology of 'Ezra' and his like, except that for the Jewish community he puts the new Israel of God, and for the enemies of the Jews the persecutors of the Church. His picture of the end in II Thessalonians is painted in colours from the crudest palette of Jewish eschatology :

It is just in God's sight to pay back distress to those who distress you, and relief with us to you who are distressed, when the Lord Jesus is revealed from heaven with the angels of His power, with a flaming fire, taking vengeance on those who do not know God, and do not obey the Gospel of our Lord Jesus Christ. Their penalty will be eternal destruction from the presence of the Lord and from the glory of His strength when He comes to be glorified in His saints and to be admired among all who believed.[2]

The eschatology of I Corinthians differs in certain respects from that of I and II Thessalonians. Some features remain, but here it is no longer said that the Lord at His Advent will destroy the persecutors of His Church. The immediate sequel of the Advent, indeed, however it was conceived, is passed over in silence, and we learn that ultimately Christ will destroy the principalities, authorities

by ἡμέρας παρατηρεῖσθε καὶ μῆνας : but these belong to the domain of the στοιχεῖα, who here are placed on the level of οἱ μὴ ὄντες θεοί. Cf. Col. ii. 20.

[1] That one might practice the Law as a matter of expediency he admits, I Cor. ix. 19–23, cf. Gal. vi. 15.

[2] II Thess. i. 6–10. If, as is possible, Paul is quoting from a current apocalypse, he adopts its teaching as his own.

I

and powers, i.e. the ' angelic ' beings (στοιχεῖα τοῦ κόσμου)
hostile to the salvation of man.[1] These are the enemies
whom He will put under His feet. The last of them is
Death, conceived as a quasi-personal power. When this
last enemy is destroyed, the Kingdom will be surrendered
to God, who will then be ' all in all '.[2] Now it may be
that at the time when I and II Thessalonians were written,
Paul already looked forward to this ultimate unity of all
things in God as the remoter goal of the eschatological
process, but nothing is there said of it. And it may be
that when he wrote I Corinthians, he still believed that
Christ would destroy pagans and unconverted Jews ; but
again, nothing is here said about it. In any case the
change of emphasis is unmistakable. The main interest
at least is no longer in the destruction of the human enemies
of the Church, but in the overcoming of spiritual powers
of evil, to make way for a grand unification of the universe
in Christ. The question is not yet explicitly raised, what
becomes of rejected Jews and pagans, or of the defeated
angelic powers, when God is all in all. But it is a question
that calls for an answer.

Now in the epistles which follow II Corinthians the
tendency already noted in I Corinthians is carried much
further. Just as Paul's revision of eschatology involved a
transcending of the absolute dualism which relegated the
whole natural order to the realm of evil, so it is accompanied
by a movement away from absolute dualism in the field
now under consideration.

First, while I Thessalonians, as we have seen, proclaims
the final and irrevocable rejection of the Jews, and this
seems to be implied in Galatians also, in Rom. xi there is
an elaborate argument to prove that their rejection cannot
be final.[3] They have been temporarily rejected only in
order that the Gospel may be taken to the Gentiles, and
when the ' full strength ' (πλήρωμα) [4] of the Gentiles has

---

[1] I Cor. xv. 23-4.   [2] I Cor. xv. 25-8.   [3] Rom. xi. 13-32.
[4] πλήρωμα is used of the ' full strength ' of a battalion, or the crew of
a ship.

entered the Church, then ' all Israel will be saved '.   Thus
the small handful of the Elect is increased by the ultimate
addition of *all* Jews, as well as of the ' full strength ' of the
Gentiles.   This latter expression might mean no more than
the full number elected to salvation, but at the end of the
argument Paul affirms, ' God shut up all in disobedience
in order that He might have mercy upon *all*.' [1]   The
coming of Christ in fact marks a crisis in God's dealings
with the human race, in that down to that time His purpose proceeded by successive stages of exclusion (Ishmael,
Esau, the unrepentant Israel of prophetic times, and the
Jews who rejected Christ), but since His resurrection
it proceeds by way of inclusion, until in the end no
member of the human race is left outside the scope of
salvation.

We may observe that the belief in the ultimate salvation
of the Jews goes along with the milder attitude to the Law.
Whereas in Galatians it is the instrument of the angelic
powers for the enslavement of God's people—an enslavement which He permitted until ' the fulness of the time ' [2]
—in Romans it is in itself holy, spiritual, just and good, but
because of the weakness of the flesh was incapable of effect-
ing its true purpose, to give life ; [3] and in II Corinthians
it is represented as containing in a veiled form the truth
plainly revealed in Christ. [4]   This indicates a less intransi-
gent attitude in Paul's controversy with the legalists, which
finds expression also in his plea for unity between the
Jewish and Gentile wings of the Church in Rom. xv.
7–12.   If we keep this in mind, then the emphasis in
Ephesians upon the unity of Jew and Greek in the Church
is seen to be in harmony with Paul's later irenic attitude

---

[1] I have tried to show that Paul meant exactly what he said, in *The
Moffatt Commentary ; Romans*, pp. 183–6.

[2] Gal. iv. 24, v. 1. The παιδαγωγός of iii. 24 is not a ' teacher to bring
us to Christ ', but an agent of repressive discipline which places the heir
in a servile position (cf. iv. 1–3) *until* Christ brings the day of emancipation ;
and the servitude of the Jews to the Law is on a level with the servitude
of the pagan to ' no-gods ', iv. 8–10.

[3] Rom. vii. 12, 14 ; viii. 3.   [4] II Cor. iii. 14–18.

in this matter.[1]   I do not suggest that there is any necessary logical connection between a belief in the ultimate salvation of the Jews and this more tolerant attitude towards Jews (within or without the Church) who at the time still persisted in their attachment to the Law ; but psychologically the two things are not unrelated.

But this ' universalism ' in the apostle's thought takes a still wider range.   In Rom. viii. 19–23, he contemplates an ultimate ' redemption ' of the whole creation.   This is no doubt connected with the dogma of apocalyptic eschatology, that in the Age to Come the whole created universe would be made anew.   In order to get the full significance of this we must recall that according to this type of thought the created universe is at present under the control of subordinate and partly hostile powers—Paul's ' angels, principalities and powers ', or ' elementals of the universe '.   Its redemption is its liberation from this control.   For minds which thought in these terms, it was necessary to ask the question, what becomes of these ' world-rulers ' ($\varkappa o\sigma\mu o$-$\varkappa\varrho\acute{a}\tau o\varrho\epsilon\varsigma$, as they are called in Eph. vi. 12) ?   The apocalyptists in general conceived them as being either destroyed or reduced to impotence and imprisoned for ever.   In I Cor. xv. Paul says that they will be put under the feet of Christ—and leaves them there.   In Colossians, however, while he still speaks of a ' triumph ' of Christ over the principalities and powers,[2] he also says that it pleased God ' to reconcile all things to Himself (having made peace through the blood of His cross) through Him—things on earth and things in heaven '.[3]   What is meant by ' things in heaven ' is clear from i. 16 : ' in Him all things were created, in heaven and on earth, visible and invisible, whether thrones, or principalities or authorities ; all were created through Him and for Him.'   Thus the doctrine

[1] It has been objected to the historical credibility of Acts that it represents Paul as altogether too *complaisant* to the Jewish section of the Church, in view of his polemical attitude in the Epistles.   But in his later phase, having won his victory in principle, Paul was a peacemaker rather than an antagonist.

[2] Col. ii. 15.   [3] Col. i. 20.

of II Corinthians that ' God was in Christ reconciling the world to Himself ' [1] is now seen to have a reference even beyond the limits of the human race, and the vague phrase of I Cor. xv. 28—' that God may be all in all ', receives a more precise and a fuller meaning.   That meaning is put briefly in the words of Eph. i. 10, ' to sum up all things in Christ, things in heaven and things on earth '.   (Here again Ephesians fits aptly into the general line of development.)   The ultimate unity of all things in God is secured not by the mere suppression or destruction of hostile elements, human, sub-human, or super-human, but by bringing them all into harmony with the will of God as expressed in Christ.   This is a conception of the destiny of the universe which not only goes beyond anything in Jewish apocalyptic, but also means a great advance upon anything which finds expression in Paul's own early epistles. We may further observe that if the whole created universe is salvable, then there can be no finality in the distinction between ' the things of the Lord ', and ' the things of the world '—a distinction sharply drawn in I Corinthians, but later kept out of view, as we have seen.

Here again the decisive change seems to be associated with the period represented by II Corinthians, though the question is a little complicated by the uncertainty about the precise date of Galatians.   The case would be pretty clear if we might assume that II Cor. x–xiii and Galatians were virtually contemporary, II Cor. i–ix as a whole later, and II Cor. vi. 14–vii. 1, a fragment of a letter prior to I Corinthians—a view which has been adopted by a large number of critics, on grounds independent of the present argument.   But though we may have to confess that we cannot have any certainty on these points, it does at least seem clear that after the period represented by Galatians

---

[1] II Cor. v. 19.   It is noteworthy that the words καταλλάσσω, ἀποκαταλλάσσω, καταλλαγή are not found in any epistle earlier than II Corinthians, except in I Cor. vii. 11, when καταλλάσσω is used of the reconciliation of estranged husband and wife.   On the other hand, they occur in important passages of II Corinthians (i–ix), Romans, Colossians and Ephesians.

and by II Corinthians as a whole, there is a growing emphasis on the idea of reconciliation, and a growingly clear expression of a belief in the ultimate universality of salvation in Christ.

CONCLUSION

It remains to show that the changes to which I have called attention—the revision of eschatology, involving the revaluation of the natural order, and the growth of universalism—can be correlated with the spiritual change to which, as I have suggested, II Corinthians bears witness.

These changes have one common characteristic : they all involve the transcending of a certain harsh dualism— the dualism of ' things of the Lord ' and ' things of the world ', of ' this age ' and ' the age to come ', of the ' elect ' and the rest of humanity, of redeemed humanity and the whole living universe.   This dualism is very deeply rooted in the apocalyptic eschatology which moulded the *Weltanschauung* with which Paul began ; but he outgrew it.

Now Jewish apocalyptic has some very noble elements, but from a psychological point of view it must be described as a form of compensation in fantasy for the sense of futility and defeat.   Historically it was bred of the despair of the world which fell on the Jews under acute and prolonged oppression.   It is in fact one way of dealing with the problem of evil when it presents itself in an emotionally overwhelming form.   The world seems full of suffering and injustice, and we, its victims, are helpless.   How then can we believe in a righteous God ?   The apocalyptists replied, in effect : These things must be in a world which, like this world, is left by God under the control of evil powers ; but in His time He will intervene and bring in His own world, and then we shall be compensated for all our sufferings and see our desire upon our enemies.   It is of the essence of the case that ' we ' are God's elect, to ' us ' belongs the world to come, ' our ' cause is the cause of righteousness, and ' our ' enemies are doomed to destruction.   The world as we meet it from day to day is essentially hostile ; our fellow men, unless they be of our faction, are not ' neighbours ' whom we can love, but enemies doomed to destruction ; the order under which we live is a proper object for resentment.   There is no acceptance of life as it is, or reconciliation to experience as it comes, for we do not meet God in it.   We set ourselves against the actual world, believing that God is with us, but not in it.   We expect of Him that He will vindicate us at the expense of all else.   This apocalyptic represents the apotheosis of a personal claim upon reality for satisfaction, power, and vindication.

There is another way of confronting the problem of evil. It is to believe that although there is evil in the world, yet it is God's world, and the sphere of His Kingdom.   His purpose is becoming effective in every part of it, though with varying degrees of intensity.   Its inhabitants are all His children, and it is His will to save them all.   In all our contacts with the world, we are in touch, in one way or another, with His purpose.   We are here in order that His will may triumph, not primarily on our behalf, but if need be at our cost.[1]   Thus even suffering and defeat may become ' means of grace ', if they are accepted as the conditions under which we may subserve His purpose. This is the abandonment of a personal claim upon reality ; it is acceptance of life and reconciliation to experience.

In principle, Paul was committed to the second position from his conversion.   But, as I showed in the preceding paper, some of the psychological attitudes properly belonging to his earlier *Weltanschauung* long survived.   He still made personal claims on life for power, satisfaction, and vindication.   He still resented humiliation, suffering, and defeat.   But in the inward crisis represented by II Corinthians he seems finally to have come to terms with life. It is no accident that from this time also we find in his epistles a revised eschatology combined with a generous recognition of the natural goodness of men and of human institutions, a willingness to claim all sides of human life

[1] Cf. Rom. ix. 3.

as potentially Christian, and a larger hope for mankind and the whole universe. Can it be doubted that this is a real development? If it is such, then the interpreter of Paul's thought should have regard to the changes which it underwent, and judge it finally not from stages which he outgrew, but in the light of its maturity.

6. NATURAL LAW IN THE NEW TESTAMENT

(1946)

THE Bible, in both Testaments, is concerned with a supernatural revelation communicated in history. The history consists of a series of providentially directed events, with the interpretation of these events by men of inspired insight ; event and interpretation interlocking inseparably. The entire sequence of events took place within the history of a single community, which passed through many phases —Hebrew clans, Israelite kingdoms, Jewish Dispersion, Catholic Church—but remained continuous and self-identical all through.

The revelation takes the form of an active relation between God and man, with man as an actor, however subordinate an actor, in the drama, and not a passive spectator.[1] This active relation is characteristically described in terms of a ' covenant ' between God and man ; a covenant being a transaction which sets up enduring relations between the parties, creates a certain status, and entails particular obligations. The New Testament speaks of *two* covenants, the old and the new ; but it ascribes to the two a peculiarly profound connection. The old covenant is not simply superseded by the new, nor is it simply amended ; it is ' fulfilled '. Fulfilment includes denial upon one level and total reaffirmation upon a new level—$\dot{a}\mu\varepsilon\tau a\mu\dot{\varepsilon}\lambda\eta\tau a$ $\gamma\dot{a}\varrho$ $\tau\dot{a}$ $\chi a\varrho\dot{\iota}\sigma\mu a\tau a$ $\varkappa a\dot{\iota}$ $\dot{\eta}$ $\varkappa\lambda\tilde{\eta}\sigma\iota\varsigma$ $\tauο\tilde{\upsilon}$ $\theta\varepsilon o\tilde{\upsilon}$ (Rom. xi. 29).

A covenant between God and man cannot in the nature of things be a negotiated treaty between plenipotentiaries. It is offered by God to man for his willing acceptance. The initiative lies wholly with God ; it is for man to respond. That response makes him an active participator

---

[1] This conforms to the Hebrew as distinct from the Greek conception of ' knowing God ', according to Bultmann's. definition in the *Theologisches Wörterbuch, s.v.* γινώσκω.

in the transaction ; it makes him responsible before God for the obligations which the covenant entails. Thus the documents, or scriptures, or, shall we say, the charter, of the covenant has two essential elements : a declaration of the act of God by which the covenant was initiated, and a recital of His demands ; in Jewish terms, *haggada* and *halacha* ; in New Testament terms, *kerygma* and *didaché*, or Gospel and Commandment. ' I am the Lord thy God which brought thee up out of the land of Egypt : thou shalt have none other gods before me ; thou shalt not make any graven image ; honour father and mother ; thou shalt not kill : thou shalt not steal. . . .' That is the twofold pattern of the old covenant. Similarly, in the New Testament the *kerygma* sets forth what God has done through the coming of Christ, His life, work, death and resurrection, and upon this follows a statement of obligation—e.g. : ' I beseech you *therefore* by the mercies of God, present your bodies a living sacrifice . . . abhor that which is evil, cleave to that which is good . . . be kindly affectioned one to another. . . .' (Rom. xii. 1 ff.). Such is the form of the new covenant with its obligations.

In various parts of the New Testament the contrast is drawn sharply between the old law and the new. But at the same time it is made clear that it is the one Law of God with which we are concerned. ' Are we making the Law of none effect ? ' asks Paul, after one of his most damaging attacks upon the ' law of commandments contained in ordinances ', and answers : ' God forbid ! We are establishing the Law ' (Rom. iii. 31). Similarly, in the Gospel according to Matthew Jesus, in spite of His drastic treatment of what ' was said to them of old time,' declares Himself come not to destroy the Law but to fulfil it (Matt. v. 17). He reaffirms the most sacred and authoritative summary of the obligations of the Law among the Jews—the *Shema* : ' Hear, O Israel ! The Lord thy God is one Lord, and thou shalt love the Lord thy God with all thy heart.' In the same way Paul, having discoursed upon the ethic of *agapé*, which is consequent upon our redemption in Christ, declares such *agapé* to be the πλήρωμα—the total content—of the Law (Rom. xiii. 10).

For our present purpose, then, we shall think of the Law of God, in both Testaments, as a function of the covenant between God and man established at Mount Sinai in Arabia in the year (*exempli gratia*) 1250 B.C., and renewed about A.D. 30 at Jerusalem. It is, of course, absurd to pretend that such precise dating is actually possible. But events which *might* be dated with precision are, so to speak, the points of concentration for a long-continued and complex process by which God's law was communicated to men ; and to think of them in this way serves to emphasize the *particularity* which attaches to all history. Events happen *here* and not there, *now* and not then, to *this* person or group and not to that ; and the historical revelation similarly was given to this particular people in the course of its own history, and not to mankind in general, though it is intended for all mankind in the end.

The biblical conception of the Law of God, then, is primarily that of a ' special revelation ', by virtue of which the knowledge of God and of His will is given to a particular community, while the rest of mankind remains in ignorance.

At this point the *Religionsgeschichtliche Schule* demands to be heard—the school which brings the Bible into the field of the Comparative Study of Religion. Its exponents point out that, whatever we may say about the exclusive and unique character of the biblical revelation of the Law of God, in point of fact there is a close likeness, or affinity, between many of its provisions and the ethical principles recognized and promulgated in various ethnic systems. Thus they adduce many striking parallels between the laws of Moses and those of Hammurabi, which were current in regions where the Mosaic code may have taken form, from a period long anterior to Moses. In the New Testament, the *forms* in which ethical teaching is conveyed are often demonstrably based upon models provided by Stoicism, and their *contents* often show so close a similarity to Stoic teaching that it seems artificial to claim that they have no relation one to another. When, for example, Paul confesses that he has learnt to be αὐτάρκης, in poverty and wealth, in prosperity and adversity (Phil. iv. 11), he is not only using Stoic language ; he is expressing conformity to a moral ideal which was original in the Stoic school. Nor does such a passage stand out alone, like a patch on a garment. Stoic morals are woven into the fabric of New Testament ethics. It is true that the robe which Christianity fashions out of the materials is widely different from the Stoic philosopher's cloak. Paul's αὐτάρκεια is by no means the same as Seneca's, because it belongs to a life which is redeemed in Christ. Nevertheless, it is a fact that elements in the revealed Law are present outside the limits of the historical revelation. In some sense and in some degree there appears to be knowledge of God which is not directly derived from His covenant with Israel.

So much, objective observation and reasonable interpretation can establish. We have now to ask how far the Bible itself recognizes and accounts for the presence of such knowledge in men without the Law.

In the main part of the Old Testament mankind beyond the pale of the chosen people is dismissed under the category, ' the nations who know not God '. Similarly, in the New Testament, Paul roundly declares that ' the world by wisdom knew not God ' (I Cor. i. 21). In the speech which he is said to have delivered before the Areopagus at Athens, mankind is described as having been in a state of ignorance (ἄγνοια) ; now at last the knowledge of God is made available (Acts. xvii. 30). The way to it is not by the improvement of any knowledge which men may have possessed hitherto, but by ' repentance '. This is all the more striking because this speech is pre-eminently one of the places where the *Religionsgeschichtliche Schule* most confidently recognizes the influence of ethnic philosophy. In fact, the greater part of it is pure Stoicism. Yet its theme is, ' Whom ye ignorantly worship, him declare I unto you ' (Acts xvii. 23).

This negative attitude, however, to the Gentile world is not maintained with entire consistency. First, we may recall a passage in I Peter—a work, it may be premised, whose outlook is notably eschatological, supernaturalist, or other-worldly. Its readers are addressed as a ' peculiar people ', who by sheer grace of God have been regenerated into a living hope and an unfading inheritance, and called out of darkness into His marvellous light (I Pet. i. 3–4, ii. 9–10). As such, they are exhorted to a holiness of life congruous with their calling (I Pet. i. 15–16). After thus reciting the supernatural attributes and obligations of the people of God, the writer proceeds : ' Keep your behaviour honourable in the eyes of the Gentiles, in order that where they speak evil of you as wrongdoers, they may observe your good deeds and glorify God ' (I Pet. ii, 12) ; and again : ' Keep a good conscience, in order that, where you are slandered, those who misrepresent your good behaviour in Christ may be put to shame ' (I Pet. iii. 16). The implication is that there is in pagans a capacity for sound moral judgment, a *communis sensus* which will lead them to recognize as good that which the revealed Law of God declares to be good.

Upon this point Peter and Paul are agreed. In Rom. xii. 17 the members of the Body of Christ, whose mind ($\nu o\tilde{\upsilon}\varsigma$) has been transformed through the mercies of God, are enjoined to ' plan conduct honourable in the sight of all men '. (The words are cited from the LXX of Prov. iii. 4, but the regulative word ' all ' is Paul's own.) Still more striking is a phrase which he lets fall in the discussion of the position and behaviour of women in church in I Cor. xi. 1–16. After giving several reasons, partly drawn from Scripture, why a woman should not go bareheaded, he adds : ' Does not Nature itself teach you that if a man has long hair, he is dishonoured, but if a woman has long hair, it is her glory ? ' Ἡ φύσις αὐτὴ διδάσκει : the *communis sensus*, then, by which pagans recognize the goodness of conduct ordered by the revealed Law of God is the teaching of Nature.

The acknowledgment of this ' Law of Nature '—for by this time we are entitled to use the expression—accounts for the valuation of the State and its ministers in Rom. xiii. 1–6. The agent of secular government is ' a servant of God for good ends ', θεοῦ διάκονος εἰς τὸ ἀγαθόν. Magistrates are even sacred ministers of God, λειτουργοὶ θεοῦ, εἰς αὐτὸ τοῦτο προσκαρτεροῦντες—devoting themselves to the work of praising the good and punishing the evil. This ' ministry ' and ' service ' to God is dependent upon the power to distinguish rightly between good and evil. It is nevertheless not directed by the revealed Law. It is therefore evident that in judging according to the Law of Nature ' men without the Law ' serve God.

There are two other important passages in the Pauline Epistles upon knowledge of God and of His Law outside the pale of the historical revelation : the well-known passages in Rom. i. 19–21, ii. 14–15 ; but I postpone consideration of these for the present, in order to ask whether the Petrine and Pauline valuation of the *communis sensus hominum*—which both authors, after all, might well have derived from popular Stoicism—has any support in the Gospels.

The evidence here is likely to be less direct and un-equivocal, because Jesus was not, apart from two or three exceptional cases, in immediate touch with Gentile life and thought. He addressed Himself to ' the lost sheep of the house of Israel '—those who, brought up in the know-ledge of God's revealed Law, had in some measure outlawed themselves but might be assumed to be still influenced by its judgments. Undoubtedly much of His teaching pre-supposes the religious tradition of the Old Testament and would have cogency for those who acknowledged it. Where He gives fresh teaching, it is often explicitly related, even if by way of alteration, or even abrogation, to precepts of the ancient Law. But this reference to the Mosaic Law is not always even implicit. ' Why do you not ', He asks, ' judge the right from yourselves ? ' (Luke xii. 57)—ἀφ' ἑαυτῶν—which might mean, either ' from your own conduct in given circumstances ', or ' from your own accepted standards '. The example given is that of a defendant who has a bad case, and who will make haste to come to terms with his opponent. There does not seem to be any allusion here to the revealed law. It is an appeal to the *communis sensus*. So is the ironical passage in Luke xiv. 8–10, which contrasts two guests, one of whom puts himself forward into the seat of honour, only to ' lose face ' by being requested to move, while the other takes the lowest place until invited to ' come up higher '. This illustration is used to enforce the maxim, ' He that humbleth himself shall be exalted, but he that exalteth himself shall be absurd.' Similarly, the parables of the Two Sons, of the Unmerciful Servant and of the Two Debtors, and possibly others, assume certain standards of judgment among men, which are true in themselves and capable of being extended into higher regions of truth. In other parables such accepted human standards are actually used to support teaching about the character of God, such as those of the Lost Sheep and the Prodigal Son. Sometimes the transition from the human to the divine is made by an *a fortiori* argument : ' If ye being evil know how to give good gifts to your children, how much more your Father in heaven ? ' (Matt. vii. 11). The rule of parental care is a universal element in a normal human outlook on life ; and it has value and significance upon the highest levels.

Such fundamental laws of life are involved in God's creation of man. There is one passage which makes this clear—viz. the passage about marriage and divorce in Mark x. 2–9 (Matt. xix. 3–9). Moses permitted divorce as a concession. This was due only to man's obtuseness —διὰ τὴν σκληροκαρδίαν. But ' from the beginning of creation ' a different law prevailed : man and wife are ' one flesh ' ; hence follows the principle of the indissolubility of marriage. It might be argued that the principle is enunciated as a deduction from the revealed Law, since the words ' the two shall be one flesh ' are in fact to be found in the Torah, but the intention seems to be to base the maxim on the *fact* recorded in Genesis—' male and female created He them '. And here it is profitable to note the teaching of some Jewish rabbis that certain fundamental laws were given to Adam in the act of creation, and among them the prohibition of adultery (see Strack-Billerbeck on Rom. ii. 14). The method by which this maxim was discovered in Genesis is highly artificial and very different from that employed by Jesus ; but the implication here too seems to be that creation itself involves certain moral principles which are binding upon the creature. It is true that the doctrine of the Adamic precepts is not apparently attributed to any rabbi earlier than R. Judah I, who died *c.* A.D. 217, and is probably a development from an apparently earlier doctrine to which I shall presently allude. Nevertheless, although the precise formulation of the Adamic commands may be late, the readiness to acknowledge a primeval law given in creation may well have been there in earlier Judaism. Accepting this provisionally, we may, without the risk of anachronism, allow the interpretation of Mark x. 2–9 which finds in it the affirmation of a moral law implicit in the manner of man's creation at the hands of God. In view of this we seem justified in giving full weight to the impression which is derived from reflection on a whole class of parables—viz. that the structure of human relations upon the ' natural ' level, relations such as that of parent and child, master and servant, king and subject, friend and friend, disclose upon examination certain basic laws or maxims which are the mirror of the Creator's pattern for human life.

Another passage seems to invite us to go further, and to say that not only the creation of man, but the order of created nature itself holds within it principles of morality. I refer to the famous passage in the Sermon on the Mount which, as given by Matthew (v. 44–48), grounds the maxim ' Love your enemies ' upon the *imitatio Dei*, and finds the imitable principle of the divine action in the observed order of creation : ' He makes His sun to rise

on evil and good, and rains on just and unjust.' A glance
at Wetstein's commentary on this passage will show that
it closely resembles what may fairly be called a Stoic
commonplace. Out of his collection of examples from
pagan authors I will quote only Seneca, *De Benef.* iv. 26 :
*Si deos imitaris, da et ingratis beneficia : nam et sceleratis sol
oritur, et piratis patent maria.* There is of course a wide
difference of ethos between such sayings and those of the
Sermon on the Mount, in that a Stoic could scarcely
speak of ' the gods ' without having his tongue more or
less in his cheek : all he really meant was the given structure of the material universe ; whereas Jesus took with
the utmost seriousness the reference of it all to the benevo-
lence of the heavenly Father. It remains, however, that
His sayings imply an order of creation containing within it
the fundamental traits of God's design for human conduct.

This view is not without antecedents in the Old Testament. It is true that for the most part the writers of the
Old Testament have their eye narrowly upon the history
and destiny of the Chosen People. There are, however,
portions of it which look beyond. Notably the book of
Job discusses God's dealing with men on presuppositions
which seem to be deliberately made broadly human rather
than specifically Israelite. The action of the drama is
placed outside the land of Israel ; Job and his friends
appear to be of Edomite or kindred stock ; the glory of
God is set forth in terms of Creation without any reference
to the history of the Chosen People or to their Law. Job,
while it has close affinities to the Wisdom books, hardly
lies upon the main line of the Old Testament scriptures.
Yet here and there in the prophets too we have suggestions
of a law embodied in creation to which man ought to give
heed. ' The stork in the heavens knoweth her appointed
times,' says Jeremiah (viii. 7), ' and the turtle-dove, the
swallow and the crane observe the time of their coming ;
but my people doth not know the ordinances of the Lord.'
And Isaiah (i. 3) : ' The ox knoweth his owner and the
ass his master's crib ; Israel doth not know, my people

K

doth not consider.' In such cases, however, it is Israel and not man in general, who ought to be guided by knowledge of God and His ordinances as surely as the creatures are guided by their God-implanted instincts ; and this accords with the general standpoint of the prophets.

But it is important to observe that the Old Testament places the whole history of Israel within a setting which is universal. God's dealings with the Chosen Race may be said to begin with the covenant with Abraham. But there was a more ancient covenant. After the deluge had obliterated the first creation, when the ancestors of the entire human race came out into a world reborn, ' God spake unto Noah and to his sons with him and said, And I, behold, I establish my covenant with you and with your seed after you, and with every living creature that is with you, the fowl, the cattle and every beast of the earth with you ' (Gen. ix. 8–10).

This passage, whatever its precise date, was written by an author for whom God's covenant with Israel was a regulative fact of history and an assured *datum* for thought. The pattern of this covenant reappears in the report of the covenant with Noah : the divine act of deliverance is proclaimed, and the obligations of the covenant declared. The writer, then, was quite deliberate in emphasizing, all through, the complete universality of the primeval covenant —all mankind, every living creature, the earth itself are parties to it (Gen. ix. 8–17).[1] It follows that the patriarchal and Mosaic covenant was made with men who were already in covenant with God ; that there is, strictly speaking, no man who is without the law (ἄνομος), unless by his own act, since all men inherit the covenant established with Noah and his seed.

Under the terms of the Noachian covenant, God offers to men a guarantee of stability in the order of creation— what science calls, or did call until recently, the ' uniformity of nature ' (Gen. ix. 11, cf. viii. 22). In turn He lays

[1] This is the covenant under which the stork in the heavens knoweth her appointed times.

upon him certain injunctions and prohibitions. Man is to
' replenish the earth ' ; he is to refrain from manslaughter
and from eating the flesh of animals with the blood
(Gen. ix. 1–7).[1]

These hints of a primeval law belonging to a primeval
covenant were elaborated by the Jewish rabbis into the
so-called Noachian precepts, which constituted the *derek
'eretz*, the ' way of all the earth ', and were obligatory upon
Gentiles. The list of sins prohibited varies a little, but it
always, I think, includes idolatry, murder, and adultery,
and the eating of the flesh with the blood (Strack-Billerbeck
on Rom. ii. 14). The earliest rabbi, so far as I know, who
is recorded to have spoken of the Noachian code is Ḥanina
ben Gamliel, *c.* A.D. 120. Ḥanina already assumes the
existence of such a code, and only discusses details of its
contents. We may therefore fairly assume that the idea
existed in the first century. It seems likely, as many com-
mentators hold, that the minimum requirements demanded
of Gentile Christians in the Apostolic decree of Acts xv. 29
represent the Noachian code, which in that case must have
been pre-Christian. Indeed, its very wide attestation in
all kinds of rabbinic sources—Talmud and Midrash alike
—suggests a very early origin. This doctrine of the
Noachian precepts is the Jewish equivalent for the Stoic
doctrine of the Law of Nature.[2]

All this, then, was part of the accepted background of
the writers of the New Testament, and we are assured that
in discovering hints of a universal or natural law in the
Gospels and epistles we are not importing an alien element
into their thought.

[1] The contents of the Noachian Code are developed by the rabbis out
of very scanty hints in Scripture, and it must be confessed that they are
disappointingly inadequate as an attempt to state the Law of Nature. But
the recognition that there is such a law justifies us in giving full weight to
passages of the Old Testament which imply moral judgments not based
directly upon the Mosaic covenant—e.g. Amos i–ii, where foreign peoples
are condemned for actions repugnant to common humanity.

[2] The doctrine of the Adamic precepts appears to be an attempt to push
back the beginnings of the Law of Nature to the creation itself. Their
content differs little from that of the Noachian precepts.

We now come to the two passages which are the *loci classici* of the New Testament doctrine of natural law—Rom. i. 19-21, ii. 14-15. The former of these states that the Gentiles, though outside the scope of the special revelation to Israel, are able to know God, whose invisible attributes are discerned by ratiocination (νόησις) from His works in creation. In fact, the pagans knew God, but did not *choose* to retain such knowledge ; and hence their faculty for discerning Him was frustrated : their reason itself was degraded from its high office (i. 28). The second passage affirms that the Gentiles who are without the law nevertheless exhibit the effect of the law written in their hearts, whereto their conscience bears witness through their reasonings. Thus it is by nature (φύσει) that the virtuous pagan acts in accordance with God's law.

Upon the question whether this aboriginal capacity to know God is actually operative, or whether it has been lost through disobedience, the two passages appear to speak somewhat ambiguously, but they are not irreconcilable. It is necessary to bear in mind the purpose of the writer in each place. In ch. i Paul is addressing Gentiles, in ch. ii Jews ; in both cases with the object of establishing their responsibility before God. So to the Jew he says, ' It is not the hearer of the Law, but the doer who is justified, and so a good pagan is better than a bad Jew.' To the Gentile he says, ' Look at the state of pagan society, and remember that this is the work of men who, knowing God, did not choose to worship Him.' In so far as the νοῦς is ἀδόκιμος it is not due to original incapacity to know God, but to wrong moral choices ; in so far as men do right by the light of nature, it is due to an original knowledge of God. In either case man's responsibility rests upon a knowledge of God and His will, which is not dependent on acquaintance with either Judaism or Christianity. Paul's argument does not require him to prove either, in the one case, that the νοῦς of pagan humanity is in fact *universally* ἀδόκιμος or, in the other case, that the pagan conscience *universally* attests the law written on the heart. I think the argument *does* require that there is sufficient knowledge of God available to ensure man's responsibility, and that there is sufficient practice of the Law of God among pagans to shame the bad Jew.

In the second of these passages there is a remarkable phrase, ' written on the hearts ' γραπτὸν ἐν ταῖς καρδίαις. In Jer. xxxi. 31–34 this is an attribute of the New Covenant, and that passage is echoed in Paul's *locus classicus* about the two covenants, II Cor. iii. 3. Is this accidental ? Or does it mean that, just as Paul, in Gal. iii. 15–22, regards the Law of Moses from one point of view as a parenthesis between the covenant with Abraham and its fulfilment in Christ, so from another point of view it is a parenthesis between the original, ' Noachian ', covenant and its fulfilment in Christ ? We have observed that in at least two cases the sayings of our Lord imply an appeal behind the Law of Moses to the order of creation. While, therefore, the Law of Moses is from one aspect the first stage of revelation, leading up to the Law of Christ, in another aspect it is a temporary expedient on the way from the Law of Nature to the Law of Christ, serving certain limited purposes, which fulfilled, it may be set aside, leaving mankind in Christ confronted by the original law of his creation.

Some such view seems to be implied in the Prologue to the Fourth Gospel. We have to observe that in the Old Testament the term ' law ' (Torah) has for a constant synonym ' the Word of the Lord '. The evangelist indicates that he reserves the term νόμος for the Law of Moses, using the term ' the Word ' in a larger sense. The Law, or Word of the Lord, according to various passages in the Old Testament, has as its outstanding attributes *chesed* and *'emeth*, rendered ' mercy ' or ' grace ', and ' truth '—inaccurately, but sufficiently for our purpose. Taking up these terms, the evangelist says the Law was given by Moses, but the ' grace ' and ' truth ' which are the primary attributes of the Word of God came not by the Law but by Jesus Christ (i. 17). It is the revelation of the Word whose course we are invited to trace in the Prologue.

First it was by the Word that the world was created. ' By the Word of the Lord were the heavens made,' says the Old Testament. Later the Word was equated with Wisdom, and Wisdom in turn with Torah. This final equation the evangelist sets aside, retaining the Word, with many traits of Wisdom, as the creative power. Next, the life thus brought into being became the light of man—the light ' that lighteneth *every* man that cometh into the world '.[1] The Word as light was in the whole world, yet unacknowledged (cf. Rom. i. 19–21) ; the Word as light came to Israel and was rejected (cf. Rom. ii). To those, however, who accepted it, it gave the right to be children of God—such as faithful Israelites (Hosea i. 10), and Gentiles who do by nature the things of the law (Rom. ii. 14–15). And so, finally, the Word became flesh. In Christ, therefore, man is confronted with that Word, Wisdom, or Law which is the law of his creation, the same which was partially disclosed to Israel in the Torah, and is known in some measure to all mankind, through conscience and reason, as the Law of Nature.

----

[1] This I believe to be the correct construction of the sentence.

7. THE COMMUNION OF SAINTS

Being THE INGERSOLL LECTURE *on* THE IMMORTALITY OF MAN
For the Academic Year 1934–5, Harvard University, April 30, 1935

IN this lecture I propose to call attention to an element in the Christian belief in immortality which seems to be insufficiently emphasized in much Protestant theology, and which I suggest is of importance in any philosophical discussion of the theme to which the Ingersoll Lecture is devoted ; I mean, the way in which individual immortality is held to be bound up with a social or corporate immortality. For while Christianity attaches a high importance to the individual, it does so only within the frame of a conception of the imperishable society, which alone gives meaning to the life of the individual, whether in time or in eternity. For Christianity the true seat of eternal life is the communion of saints, and the individual is held to be immortal within that communion.

When the question is raised, whether the soul is immortal—to use the expression familiar to Western thought since Plato—the argument may take, broadly speaking, one of two lines.

In the first place, attention may be directed to the universal or absolute aspects of the higher forms of human experience. So far as I behave as a rational being, the activity of my mind is independent of the accidents of time and space. Its processes and conclusions, so far as they are valid, are universally valid. The reason which is active is not in any particular sense *my* reason. It is Reason absolute. This absolute Reason is the ' spectator of all time and all existence '. It functions in eternity. Past, present, and future are merely determinations within an experience which is timeless. The argument then runs, that there is that in me which is in its nature exempt from time and change, and therefore from death. In so far as I live the life of ' any rational being as such ', I am

immortal.   If we then press the question, what becomes
of this ' I ' when death destroys the body which has been
its seat and organ, its immortality is conceived as some kind
of absorption into universal Mind, involving the elimina-
tion of everything which constitutes individuality.   For
individuality is bound up with the particular, the con-
tingent, the accidental.   Thus such a view of immortality
fails to affirm the permanence of individual personality.
The absorption of the individual in the universal is only
another term for its destruction.   The idea that the individual is absorbed in the Absolute as a drop of water in the
ocean is congenial to some mystical types of religion, but
it is alien to Christianity in its classical forms, for which
the infinite worth of the individual soul is a postulate.

In the second place, attention may be directed to that
element in experience which constitutes the sense of individual identity.   An ' ego ' is assumed, as the ultimate subject of the varying experiences through which it responds
to and assimilates an environment.   This ' ego ' retains
through all changes the un-analysable awareness of identity.
It is this, I suppose, that Plato had in mind when he spoke
of the soul as ' simple ' and therefore indissoluble.   Behind
all the complexities of experience there is a something
which resists all analysis, the something which says ' I am
I '.   The argument then runs, that the intense unity and
persistence of this essential ' ego ', through any series of
changes, however radical, with which we are acquainted,
justify the belief that it can persist through what we call
death.   The concrete elements in personal experience, being relative to the psycho-physical organism, may be dissolved by the death of the body, but a hard atomic core
of self-consciousness persists.

This conception of the soul is highly abstract.   To carry
over into another plane of being a bare consciousness of
personal identity can hardly be compared with that blessed
hope of everlasting life to which the religious consciousness
aspires.   An ' I ' stripped of all that makes up concrete
experience is barely conceivable, and in any case we could

hardly be interested in its survival except in the terms of
the familiar and pathetic lines attributed to the Emperor
Hadrian :

> Animula vagula, blandula,
> hospes comesque corporis,
> quae nunc abibis in loca,
> pallidula, rigida, nudula,
> nec, ut soles, dabis jocos.

> Ah, little soul, thou wanderer dear,
> The body's guest and comrade here,
> To what cold exile tak'st thy flight,
> Poor pallid, naked, shivering mite?
> Thou lov'st thy jest : ah me ! hereafter
> Thou'lt quite unlearn the way of laughter !

In actual fact, human personality, as we know it in ourselves, is not ' simple ' but indefinitely complex. In particular it is constituted out of personal relations. From
the beginning of our individual existence we throw out
tentacles, as it were, to other persons, and they throw out
tentacles to us ; and even before self-consciousness dawns
we are already caught up in a network of such relations,
by which our individuality is determined.

This process is instinctive and necessary. The impulse
to attach ourselves to others is inherent in our nature, in
those parental, sex, and herd instincts which are fundamental to it. Thus life, in any important sense of the word,
is shared life. A large part of my life is actually lived in
those others to whom I am attached—my wife, my children,
my friends—and their life is lived in me. It is fear of the
severance of these relations that gives a peculiar sting to
death, for the death of one in whom I live is the extinction
of a part of myself. You will recall Augustine's words
about the death of a friend of his youth :

I was astonished that other mortals lived, since he whom
I loved, as if he would never die, was dead : and I wondered
still more that I, who was to him a second self, could live
when he was dead. Well did one say of his friend, ' Thou
half of my soul ' ; for I felt that my soul and his soul were

but one soul, in two bodies ; and consequently my life was a horror to me, because I would not live in half.[1]

It is no wonder that simple people are always concerned with this particular aspect of immortality : ' Shall I meet again those whom I have loved and lost ? ' They are right. This is the core of the matter. It is difficult to see how immortality can have any serious meaning unless it means a permanence of relations, for without them I am not I, except in an abstract and unreal sense. The *animula vagula* is no fit subject for everlasting life.

Let us therefore lay down the maxim that the seat of life, and therefore of immortality, if such a thing there be, is not the individual as such, but the individual in his relations, relations which constitute real, concrete personality. In strictest fact I live in my neighbour and he in me, and we can hope for immortality, if at all, only on those terms.

Now such personal relations constitute a community. Every community, so far as it is a real community and not merely a mechanical organization dictated by economic or geographical convenience, is a recognition and a realization of the spiritual ties that bind human beings one to another. In a true community self and neighbour live in such intimate interchanges of experience that the common life is enriched, while the individual life is deepened and enlarged, *pari passu*. The wealth of experience changes hands like currency, and in doing so earns interest on capital. I profit by what my neighbours think, feel, say, do, and are, and I pass on to them the products of my own living ; and through this interchange I am more truly myself.

The life of a community possesses a measure of permanence going beyond the bare limits of the individual span. My experience from the cradle to the grave carries within it the experience of many past lives which live again in me ; and when my time is come, *non omnis moriar*, since

---

[1] *Confessions*, iv. 6. Translated by I. G. Pilkington.

others will live in whom there is something of me. It is no wonder that many minds for whom individual survival has become incredible have placed here their hope of a future life. Such a corporate continuity of life is not itself immortality, but it becomes a kind of substitute for immortality, in so far as it recognizes a relative permanence of human experience, as embodied in a continuous community. So far as it goes, it does justice to facts.

Now the Christian conception of eternal life, as we find it in the New Testament, has for antecedent a conception of corporate immortality not unlike that which I have indicated. The religion of Israel, as it is represented in the bulk of the Old Testament, has notoriously no doctrine of a future life. There is indeed no doubt that the Hebrews, like other ancient peoples, believed that something of man survived in the land of shades, Sheol. But Sheol is little more than a generalization of the tomb into which all that is left of a man descends after death ; and the existence of the dead in Sheol is the negation of all that life means. The prophets, who created the higher religion of Israel, appear to have deliberately ignored this primitive idea of survival, probably because it was associated with degrading necromantic practices. They would perhaps have been as little interested in the revived necromancy of our own time. At any rate they saw in it no religious value, and Hebrew religion never developed a doctrine of immortality for the *animula vagula*. The pious Israelite was deeply conscious that he belonged to a people that stood under the special providence of the eternal God. ' Lord, thou hast been our dwelling place in all generations.' It was this that gave dignity to the individual—to belong to a people whose God was the Lord. His own days are as grass : he brings his years to an end as a tale that is told : the dead praise not the Lord, neither any that go down into silence. But in those few brief years he has enjoyed the supreme privilege of belonging to a community in which the endless purpose of the Almighty God is at work. His God is the God of Abraham, Isaac, and Jacob, the

Lord who with a mighty hand and an outstretched arm brought His people out of Egypt. From generation to generation the community experiences the mighty acts of the living God, and these belong in some sort to the experience of every individual Israelite. And as he looks down the vista of years to come, he knows that his children's children will experience still more signal manifestations of the hand of the Lord, until that far-off day when His Kingdom shall appear throughout His creation, and the people of the saints of the Most High shall inherit everlasting joy and felicity. The individual life is identified with this corporate experience, past, present, and future. Everlasting life belongs to the community.

' Everlasting '—but in what sense ? For long, it would appear, only in the sense of a lapse of historic time whose farther limit is out of view. But at some point before the Christian era the idea has emerged of an eternity which is different in quality from mere duration in time. In terms of mythology, the last generation of Israel will be miraculously transformed into supernatural beings like the angels of God, fit to inhabit a transfigured universe from which decay and death are finally excluded. This, however, upsets the balance of the earlier view. While the everlasting life of the Israel of God was conceived as an indefinitely prolonged series in time, in which generation after generation takes its place, an austere faith might keep the individual content to pass away, after enjoying his brief share in the secular life of his race. But if one generation, the last, is to pass out of history into the supernatural life of ' the age to come ', then the question arises, why so great a privilege should be reserved for it alone. Shall the mere accident of living at the end of the age raise a man to a place of privilege denied to Abraham, Isaac, and Jacob, to Moses and all the prophets ? If God can perform a miracle to transform living men into angelic beings, would it be too hard for Him to perform the like miracle upon those that sleep in the dust ? So the belief arises that all faithful Israelites departed, who meanwhile ' are not ', will at the end be re-animated by the power of God, and given a part in ' the life of the age to come ', in order that they may share the triumph and felicity of the perfected Israel of God.

There is here no doctrine of the ' immortality of the soul '. Immortality as such still belongs to the community ; but by sheer unrelated miracle individual men will be given after death a direct share in that immortality, instead of being only in this life dignified by union with the imperishable society. The form in which the belief is held is as crude as it could well be : the corrupted body is to be reconstituted and transfigured. It is pure mythology, appended to a sober and realistic conception of the continuous society.

This is the background of the Christian idea of eternal life. The New Testament writers always assume that the Christian Church is continuous with the Israel of God in all ages. Called in Abraham, elect in Isaac and Jacob, redeemed through Moses, taught by the prophets, disciplined by the judgments of God, Israel has now entered upon a new and glorious phase of its age-long history, and moves on to its final consummation. It is the highest privilege of the Gentiles that they are made sharers in this age-long history of the people of God—sons of Abraham, fellow-citizens with the saints and of the household of faith.

But there has been a decisive change. In Jewish belief, when the Kingdom of God should be revealed the faithful would pass into ' the life of the age to come '—life eternal now, and no longer a succession of generations in time. Jesus Christ declared ' the Kingdom of God is come upon you ' : [1] the age to come has come. And this is the assumption of all New Testament writers. The ages of waiting are over ; God has fulfilled His promises ; eternal life is here. The language of mythology may still be used, but what is being described is no longer an eschatological fantasy, but a real, present, and profound experience. Eternal life has come, not in the form imagined by Jewish

[1] Matt. xii. 28, Luke xi. 20.

apocalyptists, but as a new quality of life here and now.

The first generation of Christians, then, corresponds on this view to the last generation of Israel in Jewish eschatology, who should be transfigured and made immortal. Upon them the ends of the ages are come, for them life and immortality are brought to light through the Gospel. But we must recall that the end of the age, in Jewish thought, brought consequences also for the generations of the past, who, when the time was fulfilled, should be called out of sleep to inherit the promises. It follows, on the primitive Christian view, that the saints of the past are now at last really alive, and no longer awaiting their redemption. The Israel of God is constituted within the eternal order, and living Christians are incorporate in this Church invisible. They are not only members of the household of faith upon earth : they

are come unto Mount Zion, and unto the city of the living God, the heavenly Jerusalem, and to innumerable hosts of angels, to the general assembly and church of the firstborn who are enrolled in heaven . . . and to the spirits of just men made perfect.[1]

' Just men made perfect ' : that is no Platonic doctrine of the immortality of the soul. It harks back to the Jewish belief that the faithful departed remain in some kind of suspended existence until, with the consummation of the age, the time of their deliverance comes and they are raised in glory. In their lifetime, says the writer, they ' received not the promise, God having provided some better thing concerning us, that apart from us, they should not be made perfect '.[2] Through association therefore with the redeemed community still on earth, the generations of the dead receive an enrichment of life, just as by association with them our life is enlarged.

In interpreting this we may fairly leave on one side the mythological framework within which the idea grew.

[1] Heb. xii. 22–23.   [2] Heb. xi. 39–40.

However its origins were conditioned, we have here a profound spiritual intuition, which in its essential significance we must attribute to the influence of Jesus Christ Himself. The Christian soul lives within a family of God, whose home is not this world alone. The ways between the eternal order and this world of mortality are open, and life is one in the two worlds. The seat of life, absolute in its quality, is the one Church of the living God, militant here on earth and triumphant above, which in and through its individual members grows into the stature of perfect humanity.[1]

In speaking of the Church in such a connection as this, I am not, as you will understand, thinking of any particular organized institution bearing that name ; for all visible churches, and even that great Church which we may dimly discern as comprehending them all, are no more than partial approximations to the idea. For our present purpose we may treat the idea of the Church as an interpretation of the meaning of society raised to its highest and most absolute form.

In the light of this idea of an absolute society we may return to the position laid down at the beginning—that the community is the sphere within which individual existence attains the status of real personality, through personal relations. Such a community develops an integrity and continuity of life precisely through the intricate interchange of experience among its individual members. It may rest upon a physical and material basis, upon the physical facts of blood-kinship or geographical neighbourhood, and upon the material facts of economic need and supply. But any society which has passed the stage of Glaucon's ' city of pigs ' has evolved for itself a spiritual life which transcends its material basis. For this enhancement of life it is dependent upon the mutual contributions of its individual members, which in turn are made possible by the community which embodies their relations. It thus builds up a spiritual heritage, in which its true life consists. It is

[1] Eph. iv. 13–16.

secreting values of a spiritual order, and the relations within which its members stand may be increasingly based upon these spiritual values in place of the primitive physical basis of association. Communities are valuable, and they prove to be lasting, in proportion as the physical and material basis of association becomes increasingly instrumental to the spiritual values of their fellowship.

When we speak of spiritual values secreted by the history of a community we must not forget that values exist only for a person aware of them, for the ' soul ', and that to speak of a ' corporate soul ' is probably no more than a metaphor. The values which society secretes must be realized in the experience of the individuals composing it. And rightly considered, individual personality is itself a high order of value created by society. A society which under-values the individual is denying its own end. States take a short cut to unity by sacrificing the individual, but in so doing they are in danger of destroying the spiritual basis of their own life. That community is most fully one, and most fully alive, where the highest freedom of the individual is at the same time the power which binds the whole. In such a community each member makes his maximum contribution to the common store, and is himself upheld and borne along by the tides of a life larger than his own. The humbler, weaker individuals are lifted above their own level by their membership in the society, and the pride and self-sufficiency of the strong are corrected by this communion with the humble.

Such a community possesses not only unity in itself but also continuity and relative permanence in time. That continuity is given in an endless chain of human generations. The generations overlap. At any given moment in its life there is a communion among its members, in which past, present, and future meet ; for every member is contemporary with others who belong to generations not his own. The old, who bring with them the traditions and memories of the past, and the young, in whom the hopes of the future reside, not merely as ideas but as determining motives leading to action, are contemporary with the mass of the middle-aged upon whom the main burden of the present rests. Where there is tension and conflict between the generations, the society is weakened and may decay or collapse. In a healthy society the interchange among generations leads to a richness and stability of life which preserves the treasures of the past while embracing the opportunities of the future. The experience of each individual holds within it in some measure the values of past and future. The heroes of his people's past exert their influence with him, and the ideals of his people's future call him to action. The individual, then, as member of a society, is capable of an experience which not only comprehends the values realized at any given time in that society, but holds within it the values of past and future. In some sort the history of the community, it may be through centuries, lives in him.

Now if after his brief span the individual passes into nothingness, then the time will come when all the values secreted by that history will cease to be. However long an historical community may endure, in the end it is dissolved, for, unless all science deceives us, the human race itself will ultimately cease to inhabit this globe. So long as it lasts, its accumulated wealth of experience survives in its individual members. When death overtakes them all, there is an end of it, unless the complex of intricate relations which build up personal life has in it something that transcends time and change.

The question then is, whether a society can be conceived whose fellowship has such absolute spiritual quality that it is not merely relatively permanent, but in the full sense eternal. And here the Christian conception of the communion of saints comes to its own.

The Christian Church is in its idea independent of every kind of merely physical or material basis of association, though it uses the physical and material sacramentally. Its fellowship is not determined by race or blood, by nationality or language or geographical neighbourhood, by

L

economic interests or by psychological or cultural affinity. In it there is neither Jew nor Greek, barbarian, Scythian, bondman, freeman. Even as an empirical society it is conspicuous among other societies for its universality, the length and continuity of its history, and the inward cohesion of its fellowship, in spite of all our ecclesiastical divisions. The worshipping Church has fellowship with its apostles, prophets, martyrs, and saints, and elect generations of holy and humble men of heart, as no nation has fellowship with its heroes, no family with its ancestors, and no college with its pious founders and benefactors. But we are always aware that in idea the unity and universality of the Church go beyond anything that we have yet realized in practice. It is constituted solely by the dependence of all its members upon the grace of God. The relations which subsist among them are determined by the divine love revealed in Christ. Every member believes himself to be the object of His love, and to be bound to love his fellow-member as Christ loves him and them. To live as a Christian is to apprehend with all saints the breadth and length and height and depth, and to know the love of Christ [1]—that and that alone is in the last resort the meaning of the Church.

Here we are in the realm of that which is eternal in its essential quality. The love of God is the ultimate constitutive principle of all reality. It is ' the love that moves the sun and all the stars '. It is pure affirmation, untouched by negativity, life absolute with no taint of mortality. Whatever is not of the love of God has the seeds of corruption in it. Whatever exists in and by His love is imperishable.

When we speak of the perfect society we are thinking of a community of human beings who live within the love of God. They are the objects of His love, and they love one another with the love of God which is ' shed abroad in their hearts '. This is the inexhaustible source of the life which they share among themselves. That life is not created by their association ; it is the condition of their

[1] Eph. iii. 18–19.

association. The wealth of experience which they share among themselves is the unsearchable riches of God, coined into the small change of individual experience, growing by interchange, but never exhausting the divine resources from which it is all drawn.

We may now apply this idea of the Church of the living God to the interpretation of society, and we shall see that it carries to conclusion those features of social life which secure a relative permanence of human experience, and hint at the possibility of absolute permanence.

First, in the absolute society all relations among its members are determined by pure love. And love is that relations between persons in which alone perfect social unity co-exists with the utmost freedom of the individual ; for only where love is, can two or more persons be completely themselves while transcending their separateness in a common life. Consequently, in this community the sharing of life which lifts individual existence to the status of real personality is at its maximum.

Again, the scope of this fellowship is universal, since the love of God embraces all mankind. The whole wealth of the experience of all men everywhere, past, present, and to come, is available as mediating the eternal life of God to all those who love Him. Everything that we have said about the participation of the individual in the historic life of the race is here true with an added meaning. The life we share is not simply that of a very long, but yet finite, historical tradition : it is eternal life mediated in history. Those who have passed out of history are still in possession of the experience of life they gained on earth. For they lived in the love of God, and ' He is not the God of the dead, but of the living, for all live unto Him,' [1] whether here or hereafter.

Moreover, within the society created by the love of God the sharing of experience crosses the boundary between this world and the other. The relations which exist among members of a true community are sublimated in the

[1] Luke xx. 38.

relations which exist between God's children on earth and the family above.   There is a reciprocity of relations, which cannot exist in human society considered in its merely historical aspect.   Within the earthly, historical order, the wealth of life flows with the stream of time, from our ancestors, through us, to our posterity.   We know that the life-blood of the past is in our veins, and makes us what we are.   We are, in some ways, better than our fathers ; but we are better than they because of what they did and suffered.   Can we only look back, and, honouring them for what they achieved, pity them because they never reaped the fruit of their labours ?   Or have we anything to give to them ?   And if we are thinking and planning for the future, when we shall be dead and gone, must we be content to anticipate, but never to enjoy, the nobler life which, please God, our grandchildren may achieve ?   I have spoken of our present experience as including the hope of the future, and being thereby in some sort delivered from the bondage of time ; but hope is an empty thing, after all, if we can never experience its fulfilment.   But if the Christian view is true, the future pays its tribute to the past, as well as receiving from the past.   In this world the child of God is beset by the limitations of individual life in time and space, but beyond this world he touches the eternal order.   In that order the faithful spirits of past generations dwell, and they too draw upon the inexhaustible treasury of life.   In their days on earth they were imperfect, burdened with mortality, to the end.   But though they died in their imperfection, they are not beyond the pale of life.   They without us are not made perfect, but in the communion of saints their individual imperfections are over-come.   And we too, imperfect and burdened with our mortality, partake in the life of the fellowship above.   Those who come after us, working out in this realm of time and space the values of eternity, will bring into the treasury of life the wealth of their experience, and we, liberated then by death of the body from our present limitations, shall be made perfect by communion with them.   It is all reciprocal, and behind and within it all is the love of God, which creates the fellowship, and can be finally apprehended only in the perfection of the fellowship.

There is here, I suggest, a clue to a problem which causes real difficulty to any doctrine of the immortality of the soul that is severely individualist in its assumptions—the problem of undeveloped souls. If the hope of immortality is made to rest upon the elevation and dignity of spiritual life in the individual, which makes him worthy to survive, what are we to say of men and women who, whether by some defect in their constitution, or by the thwarting power of circumstance, have never shown any recognizable elevation or dignity of soul? What are we to say of those who died young, and never realized their possibilities? Some minds, rather than let go the hope of immortality for them, have here and there in the West experimented with the Eastern doctrine of reincarnation. The soul, they suggest, passes from one earthly life to another, growing to maturity through successive incarnations, until it is fit for immortality. This doctrine was originally developed in a totally different context of thought. It is highly speculative. It is difficult to see how continuity of experience could be maintained through a succession of lives each of which starts in forgetfulness of all that has gone before. And the atomic conception of the soul, which in its Western form the doctrine implies, seems untenable.

The difficulty is met, upon the Christian view, first by a consideration of the social nature of personality. The undeveloped soul is upheld and nurtured by the life of the community, and its defects are made good out of the treasury of life held in common. As a child, nursed by its mother, guided by its father, taught and disciplined in the family and at school, absorbs the life of society and grows to maturity, so the community acts as a stern and kindly parent to its weaker members, and in the act the stronger themselves are made better men, as parents owe the best part of themselves to the children whom they care for. But the problem becomes a painful one when we

think with how many of its children society fails. Its
failures however are not final, if it be true that the family
of God on earth and in heaven is one, and that the sharing
of life crosses the barrier of death.

If I may turn back for a moment to the passage in the
Epistle to the Hebrews to which I have already referred,
it is a striking fact that among the figures of the past whom
the author admits to his roll of heroes there are some whom
he himself must have recognized as being very imperfect
specimens of humanity by any high critical standard.
Gideon, Samson, and Barak were no better than splendid
savages.   Their presence in any Christian ' heaven ' is in-
congruous enough, though upon the faith and courage of
just such primitive ancestors our later achievements rest.
They were not perfect, it is true ; without us they could
not be made perfect.   But in the deathless society of the
people of God they draw upon the treasury of life to which
more enlightened generations have since contributed their
experience of the love of God.   And so, in the timeless
order beyond our earth, the undeveloped soul may yet fulfil
its destiny in a wider community and a more unrestricted
fellowship.   But in fact the problem of the undeveloped
soul is the problem of us all ; for compared with what
humanity might be, we are all undeveloped, and if immortality depended upon our achieving here a personality
worthy to survive endlessly, we might well hesitate to believe
in it.   Our hope of immortality resides not in our individual
perfection, but in our participation in a society capable of
perfection.   It is capable of perfection because it lives
within the love of God.

Here it is important to consider the condition which
Christianity attaches to membership in the communion of
saints.   It is stated by Paul thus : ' If we died with
Christ, we believe that we shall also live with Him ' ; [1]
and in the Gospels thus : ' He that loveth his life loseth
it ; and he that hateth his life in this world shall keep
it unto life eternal.' [2]   It is only dead men who are candi-

[1] Rom. vi. 8.   [2] John xii. 25.

dates for immortality ; not those who have attained such a level of self-realization that they claim immortality as a right, but men who have denied self, and died to the world. If this is a paradox, it is not without analogies in familiar facts of experience.

When we ceased to be children and became men, we passed through the crisis of adolescence. The child that was, died, in order that the man might be born. More precisely, the adolescent renounced a certain order of social relationships, to pass into a new order. The child's status in society is one of dependence, shelter, and subjection to parental authority. The adult has accepted a relative independence, bringing a more burdensome responsibility, as a man among men. The passage from the one status to the other is often difficult and dangerous. It is a real psychological death and rebirth. If an infantile attitude to life survives, the man's social relations are wrong. If the adolescent or the adult tries to preserve the old, tender family relations, just as they were, they become morbid, and a hindrance to spiritual development. If he renounces them in their childish form he recovers them upon a new level, with an enhanced value.

This may be taken as a type of what it means to die and rise again, to deny the self, and so to keep it unto life eternal. It is a matter of renouncing one kind of relation within the human society, and accepting a different kind of relation. It is a real death and resurrection, though it may be no single crisis. ' I die daily,' said Paul. We must die to a world in which our own self, with its narrow and earthly interests, is the centre, and rise into a world in which the love of God is the determining factor.

The blessed hope of everlasting life, therefore, is given in an experience which is simple and need be missed by no living man. He may know himself immortal who knows that he is loved by God, and who is taken out of himself by love of his neighbour. Our charter of immortality is this : ' We know that we have passed out of death into life, because we love the brethren.' [1]

[1] I John iii. 14.

8. ETERNAL LIFE

Being THE INGERSOLL LECTURE *on* THE IMMORTALITY OF MAN
For the Academic Year 1949–50, Harvard University, April 18, 1950

THE classical definition of eternity, which governs the use of the term in Western thought in general, is to be found in Plato's *Timæus*, where he says that this world which we perceive by the senses was copied by its Maker from a pattern which is apprehended by pure reason alone. This pattern for ever *is*, without beginning, change or end. In other words it is ' eternal ' (αἰώνιος).

This quality [Plato proceeds] it was impossible to attach to that which has a beginning. So He decided to make a kind of moving image of eternity . . . namely that which we call time. Days and nights, months and years . . . are all parts of time. ' Was ' and ' will be ' are aspects of time, and we are wrong in carelessly applying them to everlasting essence (οὐσία). We say ' it was ', ' it will be ' ; but ' it is ' alone may properly be applied to essence, while ' it was ' and ' it will be ' are properly said of the process in time ; for these are motions, whereas that which is for ever immovably the same cannot become either older or younger with time. It cannot be said of it that it once came into being, or that it has now come into being, or that it will be in future. . . . All these are aspects of time, which imitates eternity in a numerical cycle (37e–38a).

This Platonic concept of the eternal, as that which is strictly timeless, was taken over by Philo the Jew. The life (βίος, not ζωή) of God, he says, is not time but eternity, which is the archetype of time ; and in eternity nothing is past, nothing future, but only present (*Quod Deus Sit Immutabilis*, 32). In this sense he comments on Deut. iv. 4 : ' Ye that did cleave unto the Lord your God are all of you alive to-day '. ' To-day ', he writes, ' means boundless and inexhaustible eternity. For periods of months and years and of time in general are notions of men, who reckon by number ; but the true name of eternity is To-day ' (*De Fuga*, 57). Accordingly, Philo defines ' eternal life ', in the one place where he uses the phrase, as ' flight to the Absolute ' (*De Fuga*, 78).

The question is, whether there is not here a contradiction between the substantive and the epithet. Life as we know it is made up of movement and change. That which is eternal (as Plato and Philo defined it), being beyond time, is ' forever immovably the same '. Can we really speak of ' life ', if we mean an existence where there is no change of mood, no process of thought, no ebb and flow of feeling, and no acts of will, designed (as all such acts are in our experience) to change the existing situation for a different one ? The question becomes acute for Christian thought, in which the concept of eternal life has been of great importance all through. It goes back to the beginnings. It is characteristic of the New Testament, which is, in fact, the earliest body of literature in which the expression ' eternal life ' (that is to say, the Greek ζωὴ αἰώνιος) is at all common, or possesses any far-reaching importance.[1] What do the New Testament writers mean by eternal life ?

The thought of the New Testament, while it has been subject to Greek influence, was rooted in Hebraic tradition. In Hebrew thought as represented by the Old Testament, ' life ' stands for fullness of earthly welfare, for health, vigour, activity, and enjoyment unimpaired by the forces of death which lie in wait for man. Not that such earthly welfare is conceived in any gross or materialistic way. On this earth man does not live by bread alone. The law of the Lord is food and drink to him. He lives the best life possible on earth when he has communion with God, for with Him is the fountain of life, and in His presence is fullness of joy. God is by definition the ' living God '. His wisdom and power in creation and His ' mighty acts '

---

[1] It occurs, as we have seen, once in Philo, and also in one passage of the Greek translations of the Old Testament, Dan. xii. 2 ; and there are rare examples (doubtfully pre-Christian) in other Hellenized Jewish writings. In pagan writers it does not appear to be found until well on in the Christian era.

in history are the manifestations of life at its highest power. And whereas the life of man comes to an end like a tale that is told, when God withdraws the ' spirit ' from him, God Himself will never cease to be the living God.

At some indeterminate stage in the development of Hebrew religious thought the idea arose that it might be possible for dead men to live again, not because there was anything in human nature to make it probable, but because the living God, who originally called life into existence, was perfectly capable of making dead men live, and had showed Himself so well-disposed to men that He might well choose to do so.   The new life would not be essentially different from the one we know, but it would be, like the life of God Himself, an enduring life, proof against death, since God would support it by His power.

At a later period, probably about the beginning of our era, Jewish teachers put forward a doctrine of two ' ages ' of the world, which made the idea of a future life somewhat more precise.   It was a doctrine perhaps characteristic of a period of history in which a large number of people found life ' nasty, solitary, poor, brutish, and short '. These teachers said, in effect : Why should you expect anything better in this age ?   In God's inscrutable decrees it is such as it is ; but there is a good time coming, when human life will be what on this earth we expect it to be but never find it to be. If you have the luck to be alive at ' the end of the age ', you may pass directly from this age to the age to come without dying ; if not, then you must wait for it in the tomb ; but it will surely come.

When this doctrine came to prevail, all the ideal aspects of life tended to be projected upon ' the life of the age to come '.   Not that it was conceived in vaguely ' spiritual ' terms.   The very crassness (to our sophisticated minds) of some of the imagery employed is proof : a banquet where supplies are unlimited, the triumph of a victorious army, a vast and unending religious festival (with all the colour, sound and drama of religious festivals in the East).   We almost certainly do wrong to the writers who have left us such descriptions if we take them with unimaginative literalness ; but they certainly show that the life of the age to come is no pale abstraction. It is genuine life, as solid, active and enjoyable as earthly life should be, without its sufferings, limitations and fears, and above all, without the fear of death. As a matter of course, it has its centre in that which alone can make the life of this age, such as it is, worth living : the enjoyment of God ; but the enjoyment will be inconceivably fuller and more vivid. Upon this view, what is most important about the life of the age to come is that it differs from the life of this age not merely in duration, but in quality.

It seems that the New Testament idea of eternal life has behind it mainly this conception of ' the life of the age to come ' ; but with this momentous change : that the New Testament everywhere declares, or assumes, that ' the age to come ' has come. With the appearance of Jesus Christ in history, His death and resurrection, the life of the age to come has been opened to men while they still live the earthly life.

It is in the Fourth Gospel that this idea is most con- sistently set forth ; and this work must be regarded as the classical treatment of the theme of eternal life. It has the actual expression ($\zeta\omega\grave{\eta}$ $\alpha\grave{\iota}\acute{\omega}\nu\iota o\varsigma$) no fewer than 19 times ; and in addition, it has the simple term ' life ' 17 times, without perceptible difference of meaning. This in itself shows that the idea of ' life ' is determinative, and that whatever implications the epithet ' eternal ' may bear, they do not in any case reduce the fullness of meaning of the substantive. ' Life ', unqualified, is for this writer eternal life ; and it is accessible to men, under certain conditions, here and now. ' He who listens to my word ', says the Christ of the Fourth Gospel, 'and has faith in Him who sent me, possesses eternal life : he does not come up for judgment, but has passed out of death into life ' (v. 24).

If such a statement is taken seriously, it follows that the character of eternal life, hitherto known as the life of the age to come, has entered into the possible range of human

experience, and consequently need no longer be a matter
of speculation, or of the projection of the ideal upon an
unknown future.   It should be capable of description, up
to a point at least, upon the basis of observable facts.   It
will of course remain difficult to describe, since it lies upon
the frontiers of our experience, and the description may
have to be in part by way of signs and symbols.   But the
evangelist has essayed the difficult task.   The *data* upon
which he proceeds are in the first place the facts of the
life of Jesus Christ, including His teaching, and including
especially His passion, death, and resurrection ; the whole
constituting a complete episode in history which in the
providence of God altered the conditions of human life
in this world ; and in the second place the results of it
all in the society which had emerged from this episode, the
Christian Church, represented in the Gospel by the original
disciples of Jesus.

The ministry of Jesus Christ is presented in the Fourth
Gospel by way of a series of selected episodes, each of which
is so treated as to attach to it a symbolic value.   The
significance of the symbol is in general brought out in an
accompanying discourse.   Thus the feeding of the hungry
and the healing of the blind have, on the one hand, their
ostensible value in the relief of bodily suffering and the
supply of bodily needs (aspects of life, upon the physical
plane), and also, on the other hand, the additional value
of symbolizing the gifts of life and light upon a higher
level.   Now in the prologue to the Gospel life and light
are said to be the two primary aspects in which the divine
Word is effective through the whole range of God's creation,
and this Word is incarnate in Christ.   Thus the action of
Christ on earth is the impact of divine life and light upon
the human situation ; and He can say, ' My Father is at
work up to this moment ; and I too am at work.'   Behind
the ostensible action is the work of God, the ' living
Father ', conveying to men through His Word the life
which He alone possesses absolutely.   As the narrative
proceeds, it is made more and more clear that the possi-

bility of such conveyance of the life of God to men depends upon a decisive conflict with the forces of darkness and death, a conflict which culminates in the voluntary death of Christ. This is a supreme example of self-devotion, and like all the actions of Christ on earth it holds within it the work of God—the self-giving which is the imparting of life by Him in whom alone life resides absolutely. That is why John constantly refers to the death of Christ as His glory, or His exaltation ; because there the characteristic activity of the ' living Father ' is at its most intense. That this self-impartation of life is successful is demonstrated upon the plane of history by Christ's victory over death in resurrection from the dead ; the light has shone in the darkness and the darkness has not overwhelmed it.

Such, in impossibly brief summary, is the picture which John has drawn of the process through which the life of God, which is eternal life, was brought within reach of men on earth. It is exhibited all through in terms of action, energy, creativity, of conflict and victory ; terms entirely consonant with the biblical conception of the ' living God ' active in creation and in history, but remote from the Hellenistic conception of the divine as a static absolute. The purpose of it all is summed up in the statement : ' I came that they might possess life, and possess it in abundance ' : and if the epithet ' eternal ' is added, it is certainly not intended to detract from the ' abundance '.

But we have still to learn what such life is, in terms of actual human experience, as distinct from the symbols through which its quality has so far been indicated. Using physical analogies, the evangelist has told us that it is *like* having abundance of food when you are hungry, or finding a spring of running water when you are thirsty ; it is *like* health for the cripple and sight for the blind ; it is *like*, if you will, fetching a dead man out of his grave and setting him free. Is it possible to go further and show us what it is to possess eternal life ?

In approaching this question it will be necessary to look again at the structure of the Gospel ; and we may begin by going back once more to the prologue. We have already noticed what the evangelist says there about the Word manifested as life and light throughout the creation of God, and seen how he is guided by this conception in presenting the whole career of Jesus in terms of the incarnation of the Word. He goes on to say that the Word ' came to His own place, and they who were His own would not receive Him '. With this clue we observe that the series of episodes from the ministry of Jesus depicts not only the impact of divine life and light upon the human situation, but also the human reaction to it in a growing hostility which culminates in the rejection of Christ and of all He brought. It is for this reason that the death of Christ, which in its essence is the purest exhibition of the self-giving character of divine life, is also the judgment of the world, since men loved darkness rather than light. The whole story exemplifies the statement, ' He came unto His own and His own received Him not.' But the prologue proceeds : ' to those who did receive Him, He gave the right to become children of God ' : that is to say (in the words of a later part of the Gospel), He made it possible for them to be ' born again '. All life begins with birth, and we must be born into eternal life. Now within the main plot of the narrative, which shows how men rejected life and light and pronounced their own judgment, there is a sub-plot which shows how a small minority ' received ' the incarnate Word ; namely, the little group of the original disciples of Jesus. It is they who are given ' the right to become children of God '.

At a point in the Gospel where the ministry of Jesus, with its effect in polarizing the two groups—those who rejected and those who received the Word—is closed, and the final act of death and resurrection is still pending, John has assembled the group who have been given the right to become children of God, and presents a scene through which we are intended to learn what it means to them to be born again into eternal life. The scene is that which is enacted at the supper-table on the night before the Passion, consisting mainly of the sequence of dialogue and monologue often called the 'Farewell Discourses'. Here mere symbolism is at a minimum, and the scene unfolds itself in terms of actual personal experience, within a real community. It begins with an act of service performed by Christ for His followers. He washes their feet. If He had not done so, He adds, they would 'have no part in him'. His action, therefore, in its characteristic self-forgetting humility, is a means by which they are drawn into union with Him. It has deep symbolical significance; but it is also a real social action, and not only a symbol, but an example. 'If I, your Lord and Master, have washed your feet, you also ought to wash one another's feet.' Or, to put it in more universal and more fundamental terms, 'As I loved you, you are to love one another.' This introduces the idea which is to dominate the conversation that follows : the idea of love, or charity—the untranslatable Greek *agape*. Those whom Christ loves are His 'friends' ('I have not called you servants, but friends,' He says). They are now to be instructed in what it means to be friends of Christ ; what it means to be objects of divine *agape* ; what it means to return the divine *agape* in faith and obedience, and how inseparable this is from charity towards one another. As we follow the movement of the dialogue, we come to see that they are not merely being instructed. In the interchange of friendly converse they are actually being drawn into union with the Christ who is laying down His life for His friends. Finally, the whole group, thus united, is lifted up into unity with God in the intercessory prayer with which the whole concludes. The initiation is complete : 'The glory which thou gavest me, I have given them.' The disciples are reborn into eternal life. That is what the whole passage means : it is a picture of what it is to be born again as children of God, and so to pass from death to life. It is, to be included in this complex personal relation, in which divine *agape* is in fullest activity : the love of the Father in sending the Son, the love of the Son in laying down His life, the love of His friends for one another in Him. The whole process is suffused with emotion : high courage in face of suffering and death, fullness of joy surmounting the sorrow of the moment, and the peace of God. This is life in abundance ; no pale abstraction, but genuine life as we know it, solid, active and enjoyable ; refined and sublimated, but with its vitality in it.

In the course of the prayer we are offered a definition of eternal life : it is to know God, the God who alone is real. In form of expression that approximates to the current doctrine of Hellenistic mysticism : ' this alone is salvation for man—the knowledge of God '. There, ' knowledge ' stands, in the main, for rapt contemplation of absolute existence, amounting in the end to identification with, or absorption in, the divine. But when our evangelist speaks of ' knowing ' God, he means precisely that system of personal relations, founded upon the interchange of *agape*, which he has depicted in the converse of Christ with His disciples. It is no less truly union with God than the ' knowledge ' of which contemporary mystics spoke ; but after all the only kind of unity between *persons* of which we have any experience is love. To be objects of the love of God, to return His love in faith and obedience and in active charity towards one another—this is to know God, and this is the quality of eternal life.

We have still to ask in what sense it is to be called eternal. Not, clearly, in the sense of abstract immobility. The idea that the way of immortality is pure contemplation of the absolute, which has its roots in Platonism, constantly presses back into Christian thought, but in the classical Christian documents it has little basis. At the same time it seems clear that for John ' eternal ' does not mean simply endless ; it does mean that which in some sense transcends the process of time. As Plato said that the expressions ' it was ', ' it will be ', are inapplicable to the

eternal of which we can only say ' it is ', so the Christ of
the Fourth Gospel says emphatically, ' Before Abraham
came into being, I *am* ' ; and that ' I am ', connoting an
existence not measured by time, echoes through the Gospel
as the characteristic utterance of Him who is the Word
made flesh. Again, in the Platonic view ' eternity ' and
' reality ' are correlatives. That which is real (ἀληθινός) is
also eternal (αἰώνιος). The temporal, being phenomenal,
is only partly real. That which is completely real is
beyond time. The same correlation appears to be intended in the Fourth Gospel. Thus, all through the
Gospel ' life ' and ' light ' are twin concepts (as they are
in much contemporary Hellenistic thought) ; and of these,
light has the epithet ' real ', and life the epithet ' eternal '.
Again, it is knowledge of God as ' real ' (ἀληθινός) that
constitutes ' eternal ' life (αἰώνιος). Further, that which
is ' real ', in Platonic thought, is also archetypal : the
world of ' real ' existence is the ' pattern ' from which this
phenomenal world is copied. Similarly John recognizes
' real ' bread and a ' real ' vine beyond the bread and
vine which supply man's bodily needs. So far he speaks
the language of Hellenistic philosophy. But the real bread
is no other than Christ, and so is the real vine. He comprehends in Himself all real and archetypal existence, for
He is the Logos. Above all, His relation to the Father
is archetypal. The relation into which men are brought
with God—their ' knowledge ' of God—is copied or
derived from the relation of Father and Son. This relation
is indicated, as plainly as language allows, to be eternal in
the sense of being independent of process in time. Their
mutual love, the glory which they share was there ' before
the foundation of the world '. It was to be resumed
beyond history when Christ ascended to the Father. But
this relation of Father and Son, in its full scope, became
actual in history, in the ministry of Jesus Christ, culmin-
ating in His death and resurrection. John affirms with
all emphasis that it was in the moment of His sacrifice
that the love of God found final expression, and the glory

M

of God was revealed.   It was at that point, therefore, that real life was actively manifested, because there the living God acted absolutely and conclusively.   If that is so, it tells us something about history ; but it also tells us something about eternity, if we follow out the thought of the evangelist.

As we have seen, he affirms most emphatically that this is the point at which, in an absolute sense, the eternal enters history.   But it is not the sole point.   For by virtue of its culmination, the *whole* ministry of Christ is the revelation of the eternal glory, and the communication of eternal life to men.   Critics have often pointed out that in the narrative of the Fourth Gospel, while there is the appearance of movement and development, this appearance is in part illusory.   From beginning to end Jesus is exercising the functions which properly belong to Him as risen and ascended Lord, the Saviour and Judge of men.   This is quite true, and it was evidently intended by the author. Christ died and rose again, that He might become for men the source of life and light ; and yet He was that, already, in His ministry.   His giving of Himself for the life of the world was already accomplished in the sign of the feeding of the multitude.   His work of enlightening every man who comes into the world was already accomplished in the healing of the blind.   In the raising of Lazarus He was already the resurrection and the life.   In each case this is true, granted certain conditions : it is true upon the condition that by dying and rising again He has entered into His glory.   That is to say, each of these events derives its reality from events which, in the temporal sequence, have not yet happened.   Each is, in some sort, a consequence of that which is still in the future, if we are to speak in strictly temporal terms.

Once again, the death-and-resurrection of Christ, as a single moment in history, is clearly marked as the moment when Christ is glorified or exalted, or ascends to the Father. Yet it is a moment which is, so to speak, distributed over a period of time ; for in the closing scene of the ministry

(xii. 23) Jesus says, ' The moment has come for the Son of Man to be glorified ' ; at the last supper (xiii. 31) He says, ' Now has the Son of Man been glorified ' ; in the final prayer He cries (xvii. 5), ' Father, glorify me now.' Upon the plane of time as a continuous, one-way process, these are three moments. In reality they are one moment : the moment at which, in Christ's dying and rising again, the eternal Word is finally made flesh and we behold His glory. And yet, after the resurrection, Christ can say to Mary Magdalene : ' I have not yet ascended : I am ascending ' (xx. 17). The supreme moment extends itself to yet a further period of time.

We have here the paradox of that which is beyond time made actual within time ; the paradox which is hinted at in the phrase : ' the moment is coming, and now is ' (ἔρχεται ὥρα καὶ νῦν ἐστίν). We seem to be directed towards the idea of a twofold activity, historical and suprahistorical ; actualized in time, and yet not dependent on the process of time, and not limited by the one-way direction of that process. The historical and the suprahistorical coincide completely at one point, which on the historical plane is the death and resurrection of Jesus Christ, *sub Pontio Pilato*, and on the suprahistorical plane is the love of God for mankind, which cannot possibly be brought into any temporal series. But because at one point the historical and the suprahistorical completely coincide, history has become capable of admitting the action of the suprahistorical at any point where the necessary conditions are present. Thus, eight centuries before Christ came, Isaiah ' saw His glory and spoke of Him ' (xii. 41). To those who (before the incarnation, as after it) received the Logos, the right was given to become children of God, for of those to whom the Word of God came it was said of old, ' You are gods, and all of you sons of the Most High ' (x. 34). During the historical ministry of Jesus Christ He gave life and light, and in doing so brought the world to judgment— and yet it was only at His death that the judgment of this world was accomplished and the prince of this world

was cast out (xii. 31). Again, after the death and resurrection of Christ, His Spirit continues His work ; convicts
the world of sin, of righteousness, and of judgment (xvi. 8),
and communicates the knowledge of God which is eternal
life (xiv. 17). Down the ages, not only the original followers of Jesus, but ' all who have faith through their
word ' (xvii. 20),—in other words, members of the Church
in all periods—recapitulate their experience, and with
them are drawn into union with God in Christ through
His self-sacrifice. Whenever a person, in baptism, is ' born
of water and spirit ', the work of the incarnate Word is
repeated. Whenever men feed upon the eucharistic bread,
Christ gives Himself again upon the cross for the life of
the world and rises in glory. Finally, at the ' last day '
the miracle of resurrection into eternal life will become
universal in its scope : all who are in the tombs will come
forth, to life or to judgment—not as though something
new and unprecedented will happen : indeed, when
Lazarus came forth from his tomb at the voice of the Son
of God, the last day was there and men saw the glory of
God (xi. 40). The same suprahistorical reality that was
manifested then works all through history to the end without itself being exhausted : for that reality is the love of
God ; or rather, it is the living God Himself in the act
of loving His creatures.

Eternal life therefore is the life that God lives and that
He imparts to His creatures in the act of loving them.
His action, though it exhibits itself in terms of temporal
events both in history at large and in the history of each
of His children individually, is in no way limited by the
time-process ; for God cannot be subject to that which
He Himself has made. The relation established between
Him and men is subject always to His creative will alone,
though within the time-process of history, and of individual
experience, it is inseparably linked with things that happen
and pass. At no moment is the life of men inherently
imperishible, for it changes continuously with the ' ever-
rolling stream ' ; and in strict fact we ' die daily '. But

at every moment our life is indestructible so far as it consists in a personal relation with God : at every moment of historical time, and also beyond historical time ; for neither the experience of any man, nor the whole course of world history, can exhaust what is in God ; is in Him *totum simul*, beyond all our apprehensions of time and space, and in that sense is ' eternal '.

I. INDEX NOMINVM

II. INDEX RERVM

III. INDEX LOCORVM

Printed in Great Britain by
Butler & Tanner Ltd.,
Frome and London